YOUR CHURCH

CAN BE

EXCITING TOO!

Sam Gordon

To: May . Maud
Shalom!
Se ___ 98?

Your church can be exciting too!
©1996 Sam Gordon

ISBN
1 . 898787 . 65 . 4

Unless otherwise indicated, Scripture quotations in this publication
are from the Holy Bible, New International Version.
Copyright 1973, 1978, 1984 International Bible Society.
Published by Hodder & Stoughton.

Front cover photograph: Novosti, Science Photo Library

Published by
Good News Broadcasting Association
Bawtry Hall, Bawtry, Doncaster DN10 6JH

Contents

DEDICATION

to

David Oram

in appreciation of 25 years ministry
with the Good News Broadcasting Association

First Word

Dr Woodrow Kroll

(General Director, Back to the Bible International)

Parents have more than a passing interest in how their children distant from them are getting on. The same could be said for apostles.

The Thessalonian believers were dear to Paul's heart. They had come to faith through his ministry and 1 Thessalonians is his letter of encouragement and instruction to them. Paul's affection for this church is understandable; they had done many things right. God was blessing them. Even the pesky little problems that had crept into the church were manageable, and Paul does not shun addressing them.

That same spirit of encouragement and instruction is evident in Sam Gordon's comments on this epistle. He never says too much; he never says too little. His insights into Paul's instructions will lift your heart and burden it at the same time. His affection for the reader is evident. His explanations of difficult issues are powerful, practical and positive. Your spirits will soar as you read them.

Reading *Your Church Can Be Exciting Too* is like being transported back to the first century. One gets the feeling that you are travelling along with the great apostle as a comrade and companion. You will enjoy reading Sam Gordon's book again and again, as often as you enjoy travelling with Paul. I commend it to any pilgrim wishing to make progress in Christian growth.

Second Thoughts

Church!

Oh, no! What a bore!

Is that *really* what you think?

Well, take heart, you're not on your own.
There's a lot of people out there who feel the same as you do.

It doesn't have to be that way, though.

It can be exciting. Dynamic.
It can be a place where things are happening.
It can be pulsating with life.

If it was down to bricks and mortar, stained glass and padded pews,
that would be it. An edifice to man.

But it's not! It's people. Real people. You!

Yes, your church can be what God intended it should be.

You don't have to go very far to find one that is. Look at the church
in Thessalonica. They were fired up, enthusiastic and keen. They
were on the ball. It was a church with the right stuff. The ideal
church. A model church.

An exciting church!

Just like yours can be ...

CHAPTER 1

A Church is Born

'they came to Thessalonica' (Acts 17:1)

What a chapter it is! It makes compulsive reading. It's riveting. Really, it's a fast moving account of where and when it all began. What actually happened?

- Paul preaches about Jesus,
- people are gloriously converted,
- the locals don't like what they see and hear,
- rent a mob is activated,
- the devil fights back,
- there's pandemonium as chaos and confusion reign supreme,
- Paul and Silas come out of hiding and do a vanishing act in the middle of the night,
- they turn up in Berea, forty miles down the road, and preach the same message to a better class of people,
- and, history almost repeats itself.

Thessalonica was quite a city. It was a place of renown - a city with a reputation. It boasted a splendid harbour. It was a thriving centre for trade and commerce as goods from east and west poured into the city. The shops and markets were well stocked with all sorts of consumer products - you name it, they had it! It had the ambience of a fashionable luxury resort.

It had so much going for it in that its location was enviable. First impressions of the city would have taken their breath away as it has been called the crown jewel of Macedonia. Its setting is picturesque with the majestic mountains of Greece, including the fabled Mount Olympus, rising behind it. Its economy was stable. There was an air of affluence permeating the atmosphere of the city which in its own way contributed to the considerable influence of her citizens. In Paul's day the population was estimated to be around 200,000 and rising. It attracted a potpourri of people who came from all over the world to settle there making it a truly cosmopolitan centre.

Today it is possible to visit Salonika in Northern Greece as part of a package holiday deal. Apart from any seasonal adjustment brought about by tourism the population hovers around the 300,000 mark making it a big, bustling city.

It was into this situation approximately two millennia ago that the trail blazing Paul ventured on his second missionary journey. He saw it as a potential springboard for evangelising the rest of Europe. How right he was!

How did he go about it? Well, true to form, he went to where the people were. He made a beeline for the local synagogue. And, when he got there, he started where the people were. In his preaching he assumed they knew nothing. He led them through step by step into the great truths of the gospel. We can learn a lot from

Paul's approach to evangelism - he used the word of God and he declared the Son of God. There were two main points in his gospel sermon: Jesus has died and the Lord has risen. What a powerful message! There were no clever programmes, he had no bag of tricks, no eye catching gimmicks to influence others. On the contrary, it was the Spirit applying the word to needy hearts.

What a marvellous response. He sowed the seed, it was watered by tears in the place of prayer, then God came and gave the increase. There were a number who said 'yes' to Jesus Christ. Three phrases are used by Luke to draw attention to the wide range of new converts. He talks about *'some of the Jews, a large number of God fearing Greeks and not a few prominent women'.*

You know, that's what it's all about. When we touch base, it's all about proclaiming Jesus and then seeing people coming to know him in a personal way. There's the joy of evangelism - lives changed by the power of God. These are the ones who would continue to turn the world upside down because they had been transformed from the inside out.

Three weeks isn't a particularly long time to spend in one place - he probably would've stayed there longer if circumstances had been more favourable. However, he made the most of the opportunities afforded to him. The message never changed - it was the presentation that differed. Four phrases are used by the historian to underline the tactics that he adopted. *'He reasoned with them'* would suggest they engaged in some form of dialogue, a kind of question and answer session. *'He explained'* means he opened up the word to them by exercising an expository style of ministry. *'He proved'* implies that he presented all the evidence to them clearly and distinctly. And, *'he proclaimed'* indicates that as he preached the word he was making a declaration of biblical truth.

And so, having watched them come to personal faith in the living God, he begins to disciple them. You can tell by the letter he wrote that in nurturing them he did a splendid job. No stone was left unturned as he invested all his energy and experience into seeing them get off to a good start in their Christian life. He covered a lot of ground in three weeks and the lasting impression we have of them is that here was a group of people who were:

- grounded in the fundamentals of their faith,
- enthusiastic and keen to get to know the Lord better,
- immensely grateful to Paul for his brief ministry among them,
- big hearted and generous in giving their money to the Lord's work,
- shining brightly for the Lord in a hostile and pagan environment,
- passionate in their desire to share the message with others.

Time marches on and the inevitable changes come. Paul has moved on. He finds himself redeployed in a city which tops the league in terms of sinfulness and which is hailed as the Vanity Fair of ancient Greece, Corinth. It has been described as a sailor's favourite port, a prodigal's paradise, a policeman's nightmare, and a preacher's graveyard. Even though he finds himself knee deep in Greece and in a situation which is less than user friendly there are many thoughts flitting around in his mind as he reflects on the infant church in Thessalonica. How would they cope? Would they be able to manage without him being around any longer? Would they be able to stand on their own two feet?

He doesn't wait to find out. He takes the initiative and sends them a letter. It is from Corinth that he puts quill to parchment in an attempt to encourage and quietly reassure them. He wants to remind them of his continued interest in them and of his prayerful concern for them.

He knows how he feels about them - but they need to know it as well! It wasn't a case of 'out of sight out of mind'. If anything, the opposite is more accurately reflected in his thinking. How could he forget them? They are family! They are his spiritual sons and daughters and they matter to him because they are important to God.

What makes this letter so appealing and so attractive? It's special because in every chapter it talks about the second coming of Jesus Christ. That's the great and blessed hope of the child of God. There is no finer incentive to living a life of holiness, no better spur to motivate us to serve the Lord. If we really take to heart what Paul is saying and believe it with a no strings attached commitment then it will lead to a deepening of our spiritual lives - we will never be the same again.

Paul never looked on the message of the imminent return of Christ as a theory to be discussed by armchair cynics who are waiting for the end of the world. He saw it rather as a truth to be lived in the rough and tumble of everyday experience. It's a clarion call to readiness - a wake up call to live today in the light of tomorrow. That's why:

- in chapter 1 it is hailed as a truth that brings assurance when our past is uncertain,
- in chapter 2 it is presented as a truth that encourages us to get our act together,
- in chapter 3 it is seen as a truth that brings buoyancy when the sea is choppy,
- in chapter 4 it is viewed as a truth that guarantees a light at the end of the tunnel,
- in chapter 5 it is portrayed as a truth that gives us the edge in a secular age.

How does he start the ball rolling? What are his opening comments? Is there anything that grabs our immediate attention?

The introduction is pithy and straight to the point. It all begins with a single word: *'Paul'*. He's the penman of the epistle. He was the prince of preachers. As an emissary to the regions beyond he took the gospel where man had never taken it before. He was Christ's flagship missionary who sailed the world with the gospel. He held city wide crusades and planted scores of churches. He was a prolific writer and was in great demand across Europe, Asia and the Middle East as a Bible teacher. Paul's vision for mission was as big as the world he knew! Unlike many of us, Paul was not guilty of dreaming too small. He knew that he served a great God who could do great things through him if he would be at God's disposal.

It's always fascinating and intriguing to watch and listen how a man introduces himself. It tells you something about him. In spite of his unbelievable achievements and his illustrious career to date he makes no attempt to enhance his own image. He doesn't need to, he doesn't have to - he is comfortable with himself and is most relaxed with a passing reference to his name. He's plain Mr Paul. What staggering humility! There's a magnificence in his sense of insignificance. Here's a man with a servant heart.

He's not on his own as he also includes *'Silas and Timothy'*. They were his co-labourers in the work of the gospel. Silas was a highly esteemed member of the church in Jerusalem. He was one of the chief men among the brethren and was credited with having a prophetic gift. Timothy was Paul's son in the faith. He was young, sensitive and inexperienced.

They are individuals who combine well together to form a team ministry. Each one has a distinct role to play so that their gifts are used to their full potential. From Paul's perspective, he is enormously grateful to the Lord for them as people. He values them for who they are and at the same time he treasures their fellowship. He recognises their superb contribution to the ministry and he's big enough in heart to acknowledge it. He is not convinced of his personal indispensability. He knows he is just one among others who make up the team and who need one another's encouragements. As a servant, he is willing to reduce his own impact so as to enhance theirs. Competitiveness and jealousy have no place in his heart. Paul is the kind of person who doesn't mind who gets the credit so long as the job gets done.

The letter is addressed to *'the church of the Thessalonians in God the Father and the Lord Jesus Christ'.* That happens to be a double address. One tells me where I am geographically, the other where I am spiritually. Two places at once - they were here and there at the same time. Our heart is in heaven and our feet are on earth!

The apostle wrote many letters during the course of his ministry but this one is unique. It is the only letter that employs the phrase: *'the church of...'* They were a company of called out believers who were enjoying a remarkable sense of unity in their midst. There was a bond between them, a wonderful feeling of affinity, a spirit of togetherness. There was a beautiful atmosphere which could be felt within the fellowship. It was electric. What a church that must have been! That's one of the reasons why it was exciting to belong to it!

Grace and peace' is the blessing he offers to them. These are the twin towers of the gospel. The order is of ultra importance. You can never know peace in your heart without experiencing the grace of God. Peace is a wonderful spin-off from the grace of God. Looking at it from a different angle, we can say that grace is the fountain of which peace is the stream.

Paul couldn't have wished anything better for them. This was the longing in his heart that they might know both blessings. Grace is something which comes to us which we don't deserve and which we cannot repay. Grace stoops to where we are and lifts us to where we ought to be. Peace is something that happens within us, a freedom from inner distraction, an internal rest, a feeling of well being, a kind of spiritual wholeness. Peace is a tranquillity of soul that frees you from fear and takes the sharp edges off your anxiety. Peace with God. Peace with ourselves. With our partner. With our neighbours. Peace with our past. Our present. Our future.

What a greeting! What a great God! A God of grace and a God of peace who came to the church in the first century to meet their needs is the same God who comes to us 2,000 years later, saying: 'Put your trust in me'. You see, Paul's letter speaks as powerfully at the end of the twentieth century as it did early in the first. God's grace overflowed in their hearts, his peace reigned in their lives. That's why their brand of Christianity was so infectious and exciting!

You can view this as only a letter to the Thessalonians
and therefore miss its message to you;

You can view this as only a crash course on Bible doctrine
and therefore miss half of its message to you;

or,
You can view it as a personal letter to you
and therefore get its whole message!

CHAPTER 2

What a Reputation!

*'For we know, brothers loved by God, that he has chosen you,
because our gospel came to you not simply with words, but also
with power, with the Holy Spirit and with deep conviction' (1:4,5)*

Did you know that the church has a fragrance? I'm not talking about Chanel or some other scented perfume! The apostle Paul called it *'a sweet aroma'* in 2 Corinthians 2:14,15.

Sad to say, in the past few years, the stench of sin has invaded some high profile ministries, obscuring the fragrance of Christ. It's inevitable, when you give the media an inch they take a mile as they ruthlessly exploit every whiff of scandal. They jump on the bandwagon and blow the whole picture out of proportion - unfortunately, the man in the street who can't see the wood for the trees writes the church off as a non-starter.

Our reputation has been dealt such a blow that we have been severely winded. The body of Christ has become a punch bag for cynics eager to poke fun. Our world may turn up its nose at the church.

That's only part of the story. It's not the total picture. The truth is, there are many more fragrant churches than rotten ones. Oh yes, there are weeds, that can't be denied. But, thank God, there are many flowers which are both fragrant and fruitful.

When I flick through the pages of the New Testament and come across a church like the one in Thessalonica I realise that there are some lilies in a muddy pond. They certainly had a reputation - but, it was for all the right reasons!

Before we look at the qualities exemplified in the church at Thessalonica as detailed in verse 3 it would be helpful to spend a moment with the apostle himself. When you read the preceding verse we are given an insight into what makes Paul tick. His mindset is described for us and it is abundantly clear that there are three important facets to his life.

Praise!

It's fairly obvious even to the most casual observer that Paul was a man with a song in his heart. Even when he found himself in a prison cell he quickly turned it into a place where he could celebrate the goodness of God. He preached about it, he wrote about it, and he practised it. Praise didn't change his situation but it radically transformed his attitude and gave him a new outlook on life.

It doesn't come easily - in trying circumstances it is not the most natural thing to do. We are the ones who make the choice to do it or not to do it. It takes a decision on our part as to whether or not we engage our hearts in rejoicing. It's an attitude problem that needs to be conquered.

Another dimension is added to it when we realise that praise is often referred to as a sacrifice. Now, where you have a sacrifice, you have a price to pay. There's a cost involved. It's not just a casual 'happy clappy' touch that we have here. It's not a light-hearted or flippant singalong. It's not even someone with an overdose of charisma. It has nothing to do with personality, but it has everything to do with Jesus and our relationship with him.

So, what does he do? *'He thanks God for them'*. That's a felt expression from the heart and it hits a note of glad appreciation. It is when we consciously say, thankyou. In many ways, we see it as a debt we owe. How encouraging that must have been for them. He writes and tells them that he feels the way he does - that's the horizontal component. But, his praise is directed heavenward - that's the vertical constituent. Yes, they would be uplifted and God would be exalted.

I'm sure that must have boosted their morale and really blessed them. The time to give flowers is when people are alive, not dead. And so he turns to them and says: thanks for the privilege of being with you; and he turns to God and says: thanks for letting me be there!

How often did he do it? *'Always!'* Did you see that? Now, Paul was no fool, he wasn't born yesterday. He wasn't naive and his head wasn't in the clouds. He knew there were problems, difficult people to handle, tensions that arose from time to time, clashes of personality. But, in spite of all their hang-ups, he thanks God for every single one of them. That's where Paul is earthed to reality.

Prayer!

He's a man whose praise is coupled with prayer. The emphasis here is on their fellowship in prayer. He refers to *'in our prayers'* - that implies they met together as a leadership team to remember the fellowship at Thessalonica. It was a first century equivalent to our twentieth century prayer triplets! How important it is for those in such responsible positions to take time out to pray - that's where burdens are shared, battles are fought, and victories are won. It was standard practice when they met together. To many Christians, the subject of prayer is about as exciting as changing a flat tyre. But, to Paul and his colleagues, time spent in prayer is never wasted time. It is quite remarkable when we realise that a year down the road these folks are still lovingly upheld at the throne of grace. They are still on the apostle's prayer list. He cared for them in the most profound way by praying for them. So, he thanks God for them and he talks to God about them.

People!

Paul wasn't on an ego trip nor was he immersed in himself in his own little world. Far from it! He deeply cared for others. People mattered to him. He had a big heart for them. You could never say that Paul was selfish or self centred - his attitude is above reproach. He looked at the church and he thanks God for them. Not only a few of them or the ones that were easy to get along with. But, every single one of them - the good, the bad, and the indifferent. It is not confined to those we like, or those who like us, or even those we would like to have like us - it's not selective because Paul is not enmeshed with the clique mentality. That takes some doing!

No church is perfect and the folks in Thessalonica were no different from those anywhere else. They were human. They had their good points and their bad points. But, they were saved by God's grace and they were a real joy to the heart of Paul. He saw beyond the externals and saw Christ in them. And, because he prayed for them, he was able to thank God for them. He loved them for the sake of Jesus.

There is a genuine warmth in Paul's commendation of them. He thinks about them for a moment and there is so much he could say - he refrains, however, and narrows it down to three tremendous attributes. These qualities underline the phenomenal blessing this fellowship has enjoyed and experienced - it's no wonder, they are an exciting group to be associated with.

They had a creative faith!

Paul is not speaking here about the initial act of faith at the moment of their conversion to Christ. That was saving faith. The faith outlined here is a faith that is active, a faith that works, a faith that performs, and a faith that produces fruit. Faith for them was not a wall plaque or a car window sticker - it was a life changing encounter with Christ.

Such was their confidence in God, their commitment to Christ, and their reliance on the Holy Spirit that things were happening in their church. They had faith to remove the mountains of obstruction and difficulty; they had faith to venture out in courageous witness; they had faith to believe God for miracles. Their faith was creative and they had something to show for it at the end of the day.

They had a redemptive love!

Labour is different from work. The thought here is of toil and of the energy expended. There was a weariness in the ministry which they felt as they broke through the pain barrier and their strength was spent. It's all about cost. What prompted them to do it?

This is the kind of love that is prepared to sweat, travail and sacrifice. Here is a love that can only be interpreted in the light of Calvary. It is a love which will pay anything, give anything, and do anything for the sake of the gospel. This is a love which counts all but loss for the making known of the message. Love is the driving force, the propelling thrust, the motivation factor - for, love always finds a way.

In his book *The Mark of a Christian,* Dr Francis Schaeffer discusses the quality that distinctively sets believers apart as children of God. It is not a pithy bumper sticker or an ichthus dangled pendulously from the neck or a gilded dove decorously impaled upon the lapel. These are only symbols of our faith. The true mark of the Christian is love. This is the most powerful of all four letter words!

They had an aggressive hope!

It's not the 'grin and bear it' mentality that Paul has in mind here. Nor is it the 'smile and shrug your shoulders' syndrome either. He's talking about triumphant fortitude, stickability, a dogged determination. It's a hangin' in there because you're hangin' on to God!

That meant when they were under enormous pressure, living in abject poverty, experiencing sore persecution, they endured. What inspired them? Hope!

Hope that it would quickly end - no! Hope that it would soon go away - no! Hope in the promised return of Jesus - yes! They were looking ahead and planning for the future. They were operating with their eyes on the horizon. They scanned the skyline and lived their lives in the future tense.

So much for them! They had:

- a faith that was alive - it was resting on the past as they looked back to a crucified Saviour,
- a love that was aglow - it was working in the present as they

looked up to a crowned Saviour,
a hope that was aflame - it was aiming for the future as they
looked up to a coming Saviour.

That explains why this little fellowship was a pastor's delight, a
shepherd's dream. An ideal congregation. An exciting bunch,
aren't they? Surely, that's the reason behind Paul's ability to say:
'Thank you, Lord, there's no people in all the world like your
people'. There are so many today whose vocabularies are bulging
with all the right words, but whose lifestyles are shrivelled for lack
of spiritual substance. These folks are, thankfully, different. In a
day when real Christianity was vanishing, either from Christians
being hunted down and killed or scared into silence, it's great to
meet people who have not succumbed to the tactics of the enemy.

Here was a church with a reputation - their Christianity was
contagious!

CHAPTER 3

Scared Stiff
About Election?

*'For we know, brothers loved by God, that he has chosen you,
because our gospel came to you not simply with words, but also
with power, with the Holy Spirit and with deep conviction' (1:4,5)*

Paul reminds the young believers in Thessalonica of three great facts in the opening chapter of his epistle. He shows them:

· where they have come from,
· where they are,
· and, where they are going.

The turning point came about as a direct result of the truth expounded in verse 4. We are elect! That means, we can be saved and know it! Here is the ground of our assurance, the bedrock of our salvation. Here is the unassailable proof that we belong to him. Because of this, the darkness can be dispelled, the doubts can be dismissed, and the devil can be defeated.

What a fact! What a statement! It blows the mind!

The opening two phrases in verse 4 help us to grasp the wonder of our relationship with one another in the family of God and also magnify the mystery of God's involvement in our lives. There is:

- an assurance - he says: *'for we know'*
- an affinity - he calls them: *'brothers'*
- an affection - he tells us they are: *'loved by God'.*

But, what does he know? What is he aware of? What is he convinced of? Here it is: *'that he has chosen you'.* This sublime doctrine is the cornerstone of our faith for it ensures that God gets all the glory for his work of grace in our hearts. Paul took one look at them - he saw the quality of their life in Christ, he saw the fruit of the Spirit in their lives, and he sensed in the depths of his own heart, they really are the people of God. God has called them, chosen them, and claimed them! In other words, they are elect!

The moment you mention election, some people are frightened and begin to panic, others are confused, more are thrilled with the sheer wonder of it all and joyfully declare 'it's a knockout'. So, what do we do? I suppose we're walking through a potential spiritual minefield but we'll pick our steps carefully. We can't pass by on the other side and pretend it's not there - it's in the chapter, it's in the word! Someone has wisely observed: 'Try to explain it and you may lose your mind, try to explain it away and you may lose your soul'.

We will never be able to plumb its depths, it's beyond our comprehension, we will never be able to fathom it in our present state. That should not, however, deter us from studying it and detract us from seeking to come to terms with it. I must confess, I can't explain it but I can still enjoy it! I'll tell you what it does - it emphasises the wonderful grace of Jesus. Look at it like this and rejoice that we are:

- chosen in Christ,
- chosen by Christ,

chosen for Christ.

Its meaning!

The words *'elect'* or *'chosen'* together with their variants appear many times in both Old and New Testaments. Generally, they could be translated: 'to pick out, to select, to choose'. It is a sovereign act of God whereby he freely chose certain human beings to be saved.

Such an idea is applied to the nation of Israel as recorded in Isaiah 65:9. Another link is established in that it is also used in reference to the Lord Jesus Christ in Isaiah 42:1 and 1 Peter 2:6. Similarly, in Romans 8:33 and Colossians 3:12, the term is associated with the people of God. God is presently calling out from among the nations of the world a people for himself, a people for his praise, and a people for his name.

Its method!

How does he do it? See the example of Israel under the old covenant. We read: *'The Lord did not set his affection on you and choose you because you were more numerous than other peoples, for you were the fewest of all peoples. But it was because the Lord loved you ... that he brought you out with a mighty hand and redeemed you' (Deuteronomy 7:6-8).* He did it in love and in grace!

Go forward now to the New Testament and what do we read? Of some it is said: *'we are chosen in the Lord ... we are chosen to be saved ... we are chosen in him before the creation of the world' (cf. Romans 16:13; 2 Thessalonians 2:13; Ephesians 1:14).* To whom is he referring in these verses? He is speaking about the same ones who are mentioned in the high priestly prayer of Jesus in John 17 - those whom the Father has given to the Son (cf. verses 2,6,9,11,12,24).

It is not that God's sovereign election eliminates man's choice in faith. Divine sovereignty and human response are integral and inseparable parts of salvation - though exactly how they operate together only the infinite mind of God knows. Any teaching that diminishes the sovereign, electing love of God by giving more credit to men also diminishes God's glory, thus striking a blow at the very purpose of salvation. C. H. Spurgeon was asked on one occasion how he reconciled God's election with man's responsibility to make a choice. He reportedly answered: 'I never have to reconcile friends'.

We should be satisfied simply to declare with John Chadwick,

> *I sought the Lord,*
> *And afterwards I knew*
> *He moved my soul to seek Him,*
> *Seeking me!*
> *It was not that I found,*
> *O Saviour true;*
> *No, I was found by Thee.*

Its moment!

When did it all take place? Away back in the aeons of eternity. Yes, it was born in the heart of God before time began, before the world was made. Before the Fall of man in the Garden of Eden, he had fallen for us in love. Because in God's plan Christ was crucified *'before the creation of the world' (1 Peter 1:20),* we were designated for salvation by that same plan at that same time. It was then that our inheritance in the kingdom of God was determined (cf. Matthew 25:34). We belonged to God before time began, and we will be his after time has long run its course. Our names as believers were *'written in the book of life belonging to the Lamb that was slain from the creation of the world' (Revelation 13:8; cf. 17:8).*

Its miracle!

This is when it becomes a personal reality in our lives. It's the magical moment when we come face to face with majesty. It's when we say 'yes' to Jesus. Planned in eternity, realised in time!

- As far as God the Father is concerned, I was saved when he chose me in Christ before the world began (2 Timothy 1:9),
- as far as God the Son is concerned, I was saved when he died for me at Calvary (Galatians 2:20),
- as far as God the Holy Spirit is concerned, I was saved on Sunday evening, 11th February 1968 in Bangor, Co. Down (Titus 3:5).

Its mystery!

Over the years it has been my delight and privilege to share in many wedding services. On the odd occasion I have had the misfortune of hearing a stage whispered comment: 'What did she ever see in him?'

I sometimes think, when I stand in glory and see his blessed face, that I may be tempted to ask myself the question: 'What did he ever see in me?' The unsurpassed pleasure of it all causes me to reflect on the words penned by James Grindlay Small:

> *I've found a Friend, O such a Friend!*
> *He loved me ere I knew him;*
> *He drew me with the cords of love,*
> *And thus he bound me to him;*
> *And round my heart still closely twine*
> *Those ties which nought can sever;*
> *For I am his, and he is mine,*
> *For ever and for ever.*

B ut, you know, there's nothing unusual about that! Oh yes, I concede that's what happened to them. It wasn't a first century wonder, however. Two thousand years later the same has happened to you and me! Look at verse 5.

'Because' is the link word. It joins what has gone before with what follows after. Paul says: 'I know you are elect, among the chosen of the Lord.' How did he know? Here's the only reasonable explanation. When the gospel was preached and the good news was proclaimed, something incredible happened. And, it only happened because the *'gospel is the power of God' (cf. Romans 1:16).*

A power which is dynamic!

When the truth of God was declared to them it came *'not simply with words, but also with power'.* This serves to highlight the powerful nature of scripture - it is explosive. What semtex is to the terrorist, the word of God is to the sinner. It is dynamite. No matter when or where the gospel is preached, God is actively working.

A power which is delivering!

The message also comes *'with the Holy Spirit'.* Only he can illumine the darkened mind, only he can quicken the enslaved will. We need God to work, but he works by his Holy Spirit. Therein lies the secret to effective preaching.

A power which is decisive!

'And with deep conviction'. The message was clear, the response was excellent. Their hearts were opened, their deaf ears were unstopped, the scales fell off their eyes, they were transformed. New men! They came from darkness to light and emerged from death to life. They became a redeemed community. They unwittingly proved

that the gospel actually works!

That's how Paul knew they were a chosen people. The same is true of us. I don't know who the company of the elect are - that's why I continue to preach the gospel of redeeming love at every possible opportunity. When, in the goodness of God, some respond positively to the message and turn to Christ in repentance and faith, only then am I able to say: 'Welcome to the family. You're among the elect!'

Charles Wesley revelled in this happy experience. His great hymn, *And can it be,* says it all:

> *Long my imprisoned spirit lay*
> *Fast bound in sin and nature's night;*
> *Thine eye diffused a quickening ray,*
> *I woke, the dungeon flamed with light;*
> *My chains fell off, my heart was free,*
> *I rose, went forth, and followed Thee.*

CHAPTER 4

Outreach is Reaching Out

'You know how we lived among you for your sake. You became imitators of us and of the Lord; in spite of severe suffering, you welcomed the message with the joy given by the Holy Spirit. And so you became a model to all the believers in Macedonia and Achaia. The Lord's message rang out from you not only in Macedonia and Achaia - your faith in God has become known everywhere. Therefore we do not need to say anything about it, for they themselves report what kind of reception you gave us' (1:5b-9a)

The church that does not reach out will pass out! The members of the young church in Thessalonica were overjoyed at the thought of their election. By the same token, they were passionate in their commitment to evangelism. They had a heart throb for people who didn't know Jesus. They were chosen in Christ - this was what gave them the cutting edge in their zealous endeavours to win men to Jesus. They had a sense of responsibility to others and a sense of accountability to God.

The God who had done so much for them, the one who had captivated their affections, the one who was their everything and their all - yes, they were debtors to him; but, they were out there on the frontline paying their debt to those outside the family of God.

That's the baseline. We're members of the global family of God, we revel in that, we delight in such a happy and privileged position. They're not, and we owe it to them to tell them of one who is mighty and strong to save. These folks were just as excited about election as they were about evangelism!

In verses 6-8 the apostle pulls back the curtain another time and shows us three more virtues of this thriving assembly of God's people in northern Greece.

Their experience!

They were men followers! For we read, *'they became followers of us and of the Lord'.* They were walking in the footsteps of Paul and in so doing were walking in harmony with Christ. As they followed the missionaries, so they followed the master.

They emulated Paul and his associates, they mimicked them, they looked upon them as their role models. Isn't that amazing! It means, Paul must have had an unblemished testimony, he must have been walking a straight line, he must have been transparent in his character. What a challenge to the rest of us for our lives are real stories that are constantly read by the people around us.

If others were to follow me, where would I lead them? Am I a stepping stone or a stumbling block? We're signposts on the highway of life, are we pointing men in the direction of Jesus? Sometimes it is said, we are the Bibles the world is reading; I wonder what translation they pick up when they read my life?

For the apostle Paul, the secret lay in his:

· closeness to Christ,
· communion with Christ,

consecration to Christ.

When they looked at Paul, they saw Jesus!

Paul was a leader and they gladly followed. The aim of any leader is to *win* souls but equally important according to Hebrews 13 is to *watch* over their souls - that's the role of a pastor or an elder in a local church.

It wasn't easy being a Christian in their day - nevertheless, they nailed their colours to the mast. They willingly counted the cost, they gladly paid the price. They discovered that whiles it cost them nothing to become a Christian, it would cost them everything to be a Christian. There was nothing comfortable about their Christianity.

The intensity of their suffering is such that it is described as *'severe'*. The pressures were enormous, the stress was at times unbearable, the strain meant they were on the verge of cracking up, their nerves were frayed, the going was incredibly tough, it was an endurance test, a struggle from dawn to dusk, it wasn't all plain sailing. Actually, their backs were to the wall as they stood at wits end corner.

When lesser men would have given up and given in, when feebler men would have tossed the towel into the ring and called it quits, they *'in spite of severe suffering welcomed the message'*.

They received the word with gladness. Here was a people who really loved the word of God. They rejoiced in its proclamation. They couldn't get enough of it. What a congregation that must have been - a pastor's delight. They were hungry for the word, they were drinking in every word that was spoken, and they kept coming back for more!

How were they able to do it? *'With the joy given by the Holy Spirit'.*
Their circumstances were not conducive. Humanly speaking, the
odds were stacked against them, the dominoes were falling. But,
they had joy! Real joy! Wonderful joy! A joy deep down in their
hearts! Happiness depends on what happens to us; but, come what
may, there's joy in Jesus. An inward joy, an exuberance of spirit, an
overflowing heart, a cup full and running over. Yes, the trials were
there, the heat was on - but, as only he can, he makes it up to them in
another way. Their lives are the richer. They are buoyant even
though all is sinking around them. God never short changes his
people. The joy of the Lord was their strength. Their experience
contained the transforming power of the Spirit and the living vitality
of the risen Christ.

Their example!

According to verse 7 they became a model church. No other church
in the New Testament is referred to in this manner, so it is quite a
unique honour to be hailed as a pattern worth adopting. They
weren't perfect! But they made their mark. Theirs is an example to
be embraced. They weren't in a rut, but they had a mould.

Reading between the lines, it would appear that throughout the
region and further afield, people were looking and saying: 'Look, see
what they're doing in Thessalonica, let's adapt it and have a go
ourselves'. Or perhaps: 'If it works there, let's give it a try and see if
it will work here'. They made the running and others jumped aboard
the gravy train. They were pacesetters for their generation. They
were ordinary Christians who had the vision to push the limits of
faith - they lived on the raw edge of faith.

This would indicate that in a constantly changing situation there was
a willingness to adapt. There was a degree of flexibility in the
fellowship as they were geared to their times but remained true to the

word. From north in Macedonia to south in Achaia, there was a real sense that God was doing some new thing. Believe it or not, but these folks were a catalyst in the Christian community. All of Greece was influenced in one way or another by the church which gathered at Thessalonica. There was something special about them. They were a beacon of light. Theirs was a radiant testimony and a shining witness as they impacted their day and generation. The thinking that governed their strategy could be summed up in three words: shake and shine (cf. Matthew 5:13-16).

Their evangelism!

So what did they do? Well, they had a message to share, a story to tell - they didn't wait for a special campaign with some big name preacher. No, they got on with it themselves! *'From you sounded out the word of the Lord'* suggests they were all involved in evangelism. They were reaching their friends, neighbours and colleagues with the greatest story ever told. The old adage remains relevant to this day: across the street then across the world. Their faith was real, not phoney. They knew how to give it away.

They all had something to say! Every member of the body was functioning efficiently and effectively. They were all mobilised in the army of the Lord. Do you know that churches grow when Christians evangelise? It is estimated that between 75/80% of new converts are won to the Lord by the influence of someone they know. Think of the possibilities and potential in your church if something similar were to take place. God loved Thessalonica, so did they! They received the word in verse 5 and they transmitted the word in verse 8.

·   It will involve a measure of preparation - we have to learn how to do it.
·   It will involve a degree of partnership - we're in it together. It's

not individuals blowing their own trumpet!
· It will involve a hint of progress - the idea is to go forward and
  not stand still.
· It will involve a note of purity - when the trumpet is sounded it
  must be with no uncertain sound. Clarity is of the essence.

We may choose to make the presentation more upmarket, we will
bring the style that we adopt into the 21st century. It is by all means
that we save some. However, the message is just the same now as it
was then. The story of Calvary is timeless, changeless and eternal.
They were sharing *'the word of the Lord'*.

They couldn't keep it to themselves. They caught a vision of a world
without Jesus. That vision had captured their imagination and
conquered their hearts. So, near and far, they shared the word of the
Lord. Like a mighty oak, the church at Thessalonica stood strong
against the harsh winds of chilling persecution and cold apathy and
spread its branches of faith throughout the then known world. They
were getting the word around. They were witnesses, telling others
that they knew Christ saves because he had saved them. They were
effective in their outreach, because they themselves were infected!

· It was a pure gospel for it was Christ and nothing else.
· It was a full gospel for it was Christ and nothing less.
· It was a plain gospel for it was Christ and nothing more.

That's good news in a bad world. It's the gospel as it really is. Oh
yes, it rang out! But they started where they were, at home. Only
then did they venture further afield. It's the Acts 1:8 principle being
put into practice.

Across the land, all over the nation, people were passing
comments about the church at Thessalonica. They were talking
about their faith in God. That was the focal point of many a

conversation from north to south.

Why? They were fired up in Thessalonica. They heard the word of God and couldn't wait until they were able to pass it on to others. They were on the ball. They were boundless in their energy. Their hearts were burning with the message of Christ. Such persecution as they endured could have smothered the flame of Christ. Instead, like pouring petrol on a burning match, the suffering fuelled a fire that exploded into even greater evangelism. That's why we can say of them they were evangelical and evangelistic. Their united testimony was an expression of vibrant, authentic Christianity in action. Someone once said that faith is like calories: you can't see them, but you can always see their results!

What an exciting church that must have been! Today, if we are willing to have a similar attitude as theirs, your church and mine can be renowned as a centre of evangelism. We can become the talk of the town when we reach out, sound out, and with the Lord on our side, get up and go out! For God has placed you where he has placed no one else!

CHAPTER 5

Sitting on the Edge of their Seats

'They tell how you turned to God from idols to serve the living and true God, and to wait for his Son from heaven, whom he raised from the dead - Jesus, who rescues us from the coming wrath' (1:9b,10)

Conversion is a life changing experience. A transformation. An internal revolution. It is something radical and causes men to march to the beat of a different drum. It's an about turn, a change of direction. It's a personal encounter with the living God and when men meet God on a one-to-one basis they can never be the same again. Their conversion bears eloquent testimony to his miraculous touch upon their lives. It was dramatic! It's an experience which happens in a moment but lasts for a lifetime. This was certainly true of the people in the church at Thessalonica.

Their emancipation!

· *'they turned to God'* - that's repentance and regeneration,
· *'they turned to God from idols'* - that's separation.

Initially they made a choice and that was followed by a change! A change of heart, mind and will - it was a change of life and life-style. There was a plus factor in that they turned their hearts toward the Lord. There was a minus factor when they turned their back on idols.

The order is of vital importance. They didn't turn to God because they were disillusioned with life. It was the character of the true God that won them over. In his light all else faded into oblivion. Salvation does not begin with giving up something, it begins with receiving someone.

They turned to one who is *'living'* - he's not dead, he's alive! They turned to one who is *'true'* - he's not deceitful, he's real!

The psalmist would remind us in Psalm 115 that *'idols have:*

· *eyes but they cannot see,*
· *ears but they cannot hear,*
· *feet but they cannot walk,*
· *hands but they cannot touch,*
· *and bodies but they cannot feel'.*

See the amazing difference in their lives. They were dead in sin, now they're alive in God. They were living in darkness, now they're in the light. Yes, they're a brand new creation. For them, and for us, it's new life in Christ! No testimony is quite as compelling as that of a changed life. People can argue theology and dispute interpretations of the Bible, but they are rendered speechless when confronted with the reality of a changed life. It is described as 'the unarguable apologetic'. They discovered, in the words of Brennan Manning, that 'it's hard to be a Christian but it's too dull to be anything else'.

· Christians are children of the living God,
· their bodies become the temple of the living God,
· they are indwelt by the Spirit of the living God,
· they become part of the church of the living God,
· and, for it, he is preparing even now the city of the living God.

Fantastic, isn't it? They could joyfully sing:

> *I'm accepted, I'm forgiven,*
> *I am fathered by the true and living God.*

Saved, they definitely were! But why? Well, their motto was: saved to serve. That was their primary occupation, their labour of love. They were captivated by Christ. The thought behind the word *'serve'* is the picture of a bondslave - one who is so devoted and dedicated to his master that he wants to be his servant all his days. He loves the Lord as his master. It is in slavery to Christ that he finds true liberty and freedom. It's a paradox I know, but it's true. George Matheson's hymn echoes a similar sentiment when he writes:

> *Make me a captive, Lord,*
> *And then I shall be free.*

The bondslave declares by his actions:

- I have no rights - it's all down to his plan,
- I have no will - except it is one with his.

Now, that goes against the modern trend. It's not in vogue. It takes an awful lot of commitment to go down that road and that's a word rarely found in today's Christian vocabulary.

- A commitment to each other in the family of God,
- a commitment to the Lord and his great service,
- a commitment to the local church and her ministries.

Commitment means saying 'no' to me and 'yes' to Jesus!

Their expectation!

Here is the climax of our faith in God. This is hope with a capital *'H'* - this is the moment we have been chosen for, the ultimate experience. What are they doing? They are *'waiting for his Son from heaven'*.

This is what makes life really worth living - we have something to live for today and so much to look forward to in all our tomorrow's. And, when tomorrow comes, we expect it to be bright and better! We know that the best is yet to be. We know that one day, sooner rather than later, we shall see the King in all his beauty. One glorious morning, the clouds will be swept aside, the shadows will have flown, and we shall rise to be with Jesus. What an exhilarating prospect - living today knowing that Christ could be back before another day dawns.

· Today, it is grace - then, it will be glory.
· Today, it is through tinted glass - then, it will be face to face.

That was what they were doing! They were *'waiting'*. They weren't hanging around idling the hours away, they weren't sitting back twiddling their thumbs, they weren't relaxing on a deck chair waiting for it all to happen. No! Rather, they were zealously working for the Lord because they really believed his return could happen at any moment.

It was impending. It was imminent. Yes, for them it was just as close as that! And, for you and me, two thousand years further down the road, how much nearer it is. In reality, it has never been so late before!

They looked forward with expectancy to the advent of Jesus Christ. They were watching for the appearing of their Lord from heaven.

They were passionately longing for him to break through the clouds. They avidly read the signs of the times and the cry went up from fast beating hearts: *'How long, Lord, how long?'*

Christ is surely coming. He's coming soon. And, suddenly! We don't know when but we do know it will happen. It's guaranteed.

When he returns he will *'rescue us from the coming wrath'.* His is a rescue mission that will not be botched. It will be eminently successful. Deliverance will be the order of the day. The *'coming wrath'* could refer to two things:

(a) it could speak of the awful eternal judgment of God; or,

(b) it could refer initially to the period of seven years tribulation upon the earth. It's what Joel called, *'the great and terrible day of the Lord'.* Jeremiah described it as the *'day of Jacob's trouble'.* Jesus spoke of it in his Olivet discourse as *'the great tribulation'.* Read Revelation chapters 6-16 and see for yourself what will happen then. It's cosmic, all hell is let loose. It's the devil and his angels on the rampage in a reign of terror. It's one calamity after another. And, it's a case of going from bad to worse, a vortex of evil, a downward spiral of sin.

Yes, Christ will come and snatch us away. The one who in a moment of time plucked us as brands from the burning will at the end of the day return and take us safely home to glory. That implies the true church of God will not enter or go through the period referred to above. Christianity is the religion not of the dead end street but of the happy ending.

They were working, watching and waiting! It's in the present tense. They were living today in the light of tomorrow. Eternity was on their hearts and the thought of it occupied their every waking moment. They lived for it and were prepared to die for it. These folks were numbered among those who *'love his appearing'*. That means:

- they were sitting on the edge of their seats,
- they were standing on the tiptoe of expectancy,
- they were waiting up for him for he could be back at any moment,
- they were watching out for him as his coming is as near as that!

Like them, our future is as bright as the promises of God. What a great fellowship they were - they fervently believed in the coming of the Lord. They were excited about eschatology!

> *I am waiting for the coming,*
> *of the Lord who died for me;*
> *Oh, his words have thrilled my spirit,*
> *I will come again for thee.*
> *I can almost hear his foot fall*
> *on the threshold of the door,*
> *And my heart, my heart is longing -*
> *to be with him evermore.*

CHAPTER 6

An all round ministry (1)

'You know, brothers, that our visit to you was not a failure. We had previously suffered and been insulted in Philippi, as you know, but with the help of our God we dared to tell you his gospel in spite of strong opposition. For the appeal we make does not spring from error or impure motives, nor are we trying to trick you. On the contrary, we speak as men approved by God to be entrusted with the gospel. We are not trying to please men but God, who tests our hearts. You know we never used flattery, nor did we put on a mask to cover up greed - God is our witness. We were not looking for praise from men, not from you or anyone else' (2:1-6)

Every pastor is given the command: *'Do the work of an evangelist'*. That's evidently what Paul did as it was through his faithful preaching that the church in Thessalonica was founded. And, it was through his faithful pastoring that the infant church progressed down the road to spiritual maturity.

Alan Redpath has observed, 'The conversion of a soul is the miracle of a moment, the manufacture of a saint is the task of a lifetime'. Therein lies the difference between commitment to Christ and consecration to Christ. It's one thing to start the race, it's quite another matter to keep on track and cross the finishing line. Sadly, so many appear to fall out on the last lap.

As we begin to look at the second chapter of Paul's stirring epistle Paul is reminding them of the kind of ministry he exercised among them. He paints five pictures of his ministry on the canvas of the word of God. What are they? We see:

· his rejoicing as a reaper in verse 1
· his purpose as a preacher in verses 2-6
· his nature as a nurse in verses 7,8
· his saintliness as a servant in verses 9,10
· his faithfulness as a father in verses 11,12.

That's a thumbnail sketch of his ministry. He has given us a vignette of the role he occupied when he was with them. He exercised in the words of C. H. Spurgeon, *'an all round ministry'*. Paul is here defending his life and labours among them. He is standing at the crease and is batting on the front foot. The problem had arisen that some people were pointing a finger at him, others were spreading malicious stories about him, a few were trying to undermine his ministry. And so, he moves to quell the rumours and reassure the church. He voluntarily goes on the record and says: 'let the facts speak for themselves!'

What a thrilling story it is! It's front page news. The first century Billy Graham spent three weeks with them and as a result of his efforts a church had been started. He is oozing with confidence for he knows his track record speaks for itself. He doesn't juggle with the statistics to make them look better than they really are. He says quite categorically that in spite of what other people may say (including the cynics and critics) they knew his visit to them was a runaway success. It was resoundingly positive.

By any stretch of the imagination, it was certainly not a failure. You can read all about it in Acts 17. It's a fantastic account of God at work. The seed of the word was sown, it bore fruit, and the harvest was gathered in. As I have indicated earlier in our study, he talked about the various groupings of people who found the Lord - he asked the penetrating question, 'what's that?' It's God giving the increase! His labours were well rewarded. He could look back with no tinge of sadness, no hint of regret. He was buoyant because God had performed a series of miracles in Northern Greece. The apostle says: *'it was worth it all, it wasn't in vain'.*

Remember the sentiments of the saintly Samuel Rutherford writing from his prison cell in the granite city of Aberdeen. He was reflecting on his pastoral charge in Galloway in south-west Scotland when he wrote:

> *Fair Anwoth by the Solway, to me thou still art dear,*
> *E'en on the verge of heaven, I drop for thee a tear,*
> *Oh, if one soul from Anwoth, meet me at God's right hand,*
> *My heaven will be two heavens, in Immanuel's land.*

In verse 2 Paul gives us quite a remarkable insight into what life was like for a travelling preacher in the first century. They were often hunted and hounded. They were frequently beaten up and left on the roadside. They were often brought to court to face trumped up charges. Regularly they were thrown out of town and labelled as undesirables. Someone has said that if you were to trace Paul's journeys in the first century, it would be like tracking the path of a wounded deer running from a hunter, leaving one bloody trail after another. This was Europe two thousand years ago.

His persecution!

He explains and exposes what happened at Philippi. They had been physically abused, they had suffered badly at the hands of others, they had been grossly insulted, they had experienced deprivation, they underwent systematic mental torture, they went through the mill. And again, he says, *'as you know'.*

In spite of all the harassment and humiliation they encountered, they pressed on! They battled on, they soldiered on. They resolutely moved ahead. That's how they happened to find themselves in Thessalonica.

In Acts 16:40 they brought comfort to the saints at Philippi and they encouraged them. In Acts 17:1-10 they brought Christ to the sinner in Thessalonica and evangelised them.

How were they able to keep going? What was their secret? The answer is seen in a fresh new light in the middle of verse 2.

His power!

It was with *'the help of our God'.* They were not depending or relying on past success, on academic ability, nor on the arm of flesh. Their strength lay in God. He enabled them and undertook for them. And so with bravery and boldness they preached Jesus. The wonderful thing about it is this, God never let them down. Not once! How could he?

There's a mighty phrase employed in verse 2 which reinforces the kind of man Paul really was. It says, *'we dared to tell you'* - that means, they dared for the Lord! The odds were stacked against them, they were deep in enemy territory, they were on the frontline of battle, they were operating in a stronghold of Satan, but still they dared.

They faced the opposition head on. It was an eyeball to eyeball confrontation. They pulled no punches as they squared up to them. They took their hands out of their pockets, rolled up their sleeves, and knocked the enemy out cold!

Bold, yes they were! Courageous, yes they were! Men, ordinary
men, yes they were! But, they were men with a heart for God and a
burning passion aflame in their breast. Their philosophy was, there's
no gain without pain, no crown without a cross. They saw today in
the light of tomorrow.

Again, you are maybe saying: 'that's all very well, more power to
their elbow, it's fine for them, but why did they do it?' The answer
is found in verse 4.

His privilege!

Paul has a profound sense of privilege that leaves him overwhelmed.
He sees himself as a steward entrusted with a priceless and valuable
treasure. He can't understand it fully, he can't explain it
satisfactorily, it leaves him spellbound and lost for words. To think
that God has hand picked him and counted him worthy to put him
into the ministry - well, the thrill of that has never left him! He has a
great sense of awe and wonder at his calling in life. *'To be allowed
and approved of God'* is something that leaves him out of breath.

He had passed the divine selection process having been vetted by the
Spirit of God. He enjoyed the backing and blessing of the Lord. He
had been tested many times but on every occasion he passed with
flying colours. He knew how to handle himself when disappointment
came (remember John Mark left him for greener pastures); he had
often encountered danger and diced with death (remember the stoning
at Lystra); he knew the pressure of dealing with internal wrangling
and disputes, politics in Christian work, and he came out at the other
end untainted and untarnished (remember the council at Jerusalem).

Yes, here was a man who had been sorely tried, but who could be trusted! He was an individual who had been given the benefit of God's approval. God endorsed him and gave him a glowing reference. You can't get a better commendation than that! God was with him. God was for him.

That's why he can face the enemy. That's why he can walk down the Main Street with his head held high. Come what may, he knows that God has vindicated him as a man and wonderfully blessed his ministry. He's not on an ego trip, he's not flaunting himself, he's not a superstar. No, he's still Paul, famed for his humility. Just plain Paul whose trust is fixed in God.

His preaching!

Anything he said in the course of his spoken ministry he is happy to stand over. It was the gospel of God's dear Son. There was no other message, no other theme. There was no human rhetoric or opinion. The gospel was the foundation upon which the apostle built his exhortations and reproofs. He never got side-tracked nor did he allow others to lead him into bypath meadow. All he told them about was the gospel of the sovereign and saving grace of God.

He pleaded with them in verse 3 to accept it for three reasons:

· the facts are there and the facts are true,
· there were no sensual undertones in what they said or did,
· they never attempted to pull the wool over other people's eyes.

And, he goes on to affirm that:

· men didn't matter (v. 4b) - he wasn't a man pleaser. He never attempted to play to the gallery and be of all men most plausible. He had no desire to impress them. There was nothing smooth about his tongue;

money didn't matter (v. 5) - he wasn't in it for what he could get out of it. He never attempted to fleece the flock or exploit them in any way. He didn't have one hand around their shoulders and the other in their pockets;

merit didn't matter (v. 6) - he wasn't interested in being centre stage hogging the limelight. He had no hidden agenda either for them or himself. He was the epitome of transparency as he wasn't afraid to divulge his struggles and weaknesses - he knew that his humanness was the very avenue through which Christ's work would be revealed.

His was not a mercenary mentality. His tactics were not those of a guerrilla soldier. He was not a shady character from the underworld. His was not the hit and run mindset. His was not a covert deployment. Certainly not!

When you analyse Paul's defence in verses 1-6 it is abundantly clear that he wasn't preaching just for the good of his health, nor was he in it to line his own pockets. There was no hypocrisy, no hype. He wasn't preaching for anything or anyone but the Lord. He was all that mattered. God's verdict was all that counted. Here was a man who cared supremely what God thought of his ministry. That's the reason he is the man he is!

Paul loved the truth and he loved the task in hand. He loved the word of the Lord and he was dedicated to the Lord of the word.

CHAPTER 7

An all round ministry (2)

'As apostles of Christ we could have been a burden to you, but we were gentle among you, like a mother caring for her little children. We loved you so much that we were delighted to share with you not only the gospel of God but our lives as well, because you had become so dear to us. Surely you remember, brothers, our toil and hardship; we worked night and day in order not to be a burden to anyone while we preached the gospel of God to you. You are witnesses, and so is God, of how holy, righteous and blameless we were among you who believed. For you know that we dealt with each of you as a father deals with his own children, encouraging, comforting and urging you to live lives worthy of God, who calls you into his kingdom and glory' (2:7-12)

Good leadership is so important in every situation. Today you can attend many conferences, read a wide variety of books, watch an enormous selection of videos - you can do so much, you can hear so much - all on the subject of leadership and how to be a better one!

A good leader according to Paul is someone who inspires influence, who takes the initiative, who sees the need and gets the job done. In this section of his letter there are a few more qualities detailed:

· he should be sensitive to the needs of others (v. 7)
· he should have an affection for people (v. 8)
· he should have an authentic lifestyle (vs. 9,10)
· he should be enthusiastic in his affirmation of others (v. 11).

Here is a profile of an effective servant of God.

In verses 7 and 8 the picture is that of a mother and her children and the underlying thought is one of gentleness. Here we see the tender loving care he showed towards them. He was respected as a man of his time. To some people, he may have had a macho image. Yet, here he is saying, 'we mothered you'.

It was tender!

One translation uses the term *'cherishing'* which means *'to warm'*. That's what Paul did - he warmed their hearts, he ignited the spark in their lives. Another picture is hinted at in Deuteronomy 22:6 where we read of the mother bird covering her young - these young converts were in his arms and close to his heart. He's not aloof, distant or unapproachable. He's in there with them, loving them. It's selfless and sacrificial. He is fully aware of their needs and he sought to meet them. Here's a man with a mother's heart. Charles Swindoll reminds us that 'the pulpit shouldn't be a stainless steel milk dispenser but a rocking chair, where the pastor lovingly nurses the church.'

It was devoted!

'We loved you so much ... you had become so dear to us'. That's affection at its finest and best. He yearned for them, he had a big heart for them. Just like a mother yearning over her child as in Job 3:21 he was concerned for them. They were his pride and joy. He didn't turn them over to baby sitters or child minders, he cared for

them himself. He felt deeply for them because they had won his heart. Don't get the idea from Paul's loving language that he was a spiritual softie; he was a warrior for the gospel.

It was genuine!

Yes, they were happy to share the gospel with them, but surpassing that, Paul was willing to wrap his life up in theirs. He was so motivated by love that nothing was too much trouble to him. He gave everything. He held nothing back. It was unreserved abandonment. He was one hundred percent committed to them. Paul was more than just a vending machine for the truth - he actually imparted his life to them. He stayed with them and fleshed out the gospel he preached. His whole life incarnated the love of God. That's what real ministry is - it's not lobbing instructions from the sidelines to those who are struggling in the game of life. It's being in there with them!

When we go further down the chapter to verses 9 and 10 we are brought face to face with his saintliness as a servant. It is apparent that he knew exactly what he was doing and it shows itself in many different ways. He got it right from at least three angles.

His preaching is right!

The only message he shared with them is what he calls *'the gospel of God'*. It is the good news, the best news, the only news worth listening to. It is the evangel. According to 1 Corinthians 15 it incorporated three fundamental truths:

- Christ died for our sins,
- Christ was buried,
- Christ was raised again on the third day.

It was a solidly biblical message. It was the word of the Lord.

His priorities are right!

He didn't want to be a burden to them financially so he plied his trade as a tentmaker by day and preached by night. He was tireless in his efforts as he expended incredible amounts of energy. He just worked himself to the bone. Oh yes, it was a real struggle at times, there were many tears, but he did it all for them. It wasn't an easy option for him, not an alternative lifestyle. It certainly wasn't a cop-out. All of this is an indication that his priorities were spot on. He knows what he is doing is right so he gets on with it. He knows where he is going and so he gets there.

His profession is right!

He's a brave man. What a claim for any man to make! He says they know it, and God knows it! He is a man of unquestioned integrity as he tells them how it was when he was privileged to be with them.

·   He is holy. That's his conduct in relation to God. He is a man of piety. The Old Testament speaks of the *beauty of holiness*. And when you look at Paul you see someone who knows to whom he belongs and is perfectly satisfied. He was single minded in that he was sold out to Jesus.

·   He is righteous. That's his conduct in relation to men. He was a just man. He behaved himself in such a manner that his whole life was above and beyond reproach. He didn't leave himself open for justified criticism as he was upright in all aspects of his public ministry.

·   He is blameless. That's his conduct in relation to self. He wasn't sinless, he wasn't perfect, he wasn't without fault. He never said that he was! But, he was open, honest and transparent.

As we consider verses 11 and 12 we have a beautiful picture emerging of his relationship with them being likened to a father and his children. He has a paternal instinct and ensures they get the best of individual attention. Each one was important to him. They really mattered to him as he sought to deal with them on a personal basis. What did he do?

He encouraged them!

He lifted their hearts. People get discouraged so easily so his ministry to them was one of support. He gave them a listening ear and an understanding heart. He got alongside them and made them feel better. It's the Barnabas syndrome being worked out in the context of a local church family. Isn't it more logical to give flowers to people when they are living rather than waiting until they are dead?

He comforted them!

He certainly didn't pamper or mollycoddle them. Because of his unique style in ministering into their situation he made them want to do better in themselves. He urged them to keep on trying, to hang in there, to hold on tight. He sought to bring out the best in them.

He urged them!

This means he testified to them from his own experience. It's the principle established in 2 Corinthians 1:3,4 being put into practice. He shared with them what had happened to him. He followed the example of the old prophet Ezekiel in that he sat where they sat. Remember Corrie Ten Boom! When her sister Betsy was dying in

Ravensbruck she uttered a sentence that has travelled around the world. She said, 'There is no pit that Christ is not deeper still'. Another profound comment came from her lips of equal worth when she said, 'They will listen to us because we have been here'.

So true, isn't it! God has no problems, only plans!

He could empathise with them. He knew what made them tick. That's why he urged them.

Here was a leader at work. He led by example and he led by encouragement. Why did he do it? What was his ultimate goal? It was so that they *might live lives worthy of God'*. They needed to learn how to walk. In those early stages of 'finding their feet' he was always available to them as a father.

The importance of this experience is underlined with the reminder that he is the one *'who calls you'*. It's in the present tense. They have been called to salvation. Now he is calling them to a life of obedience and holiness. In chapter one of his letter we see them converted, here we see them growing in grace and going on with the Lord. Whether we preach from a pulpit on a Sunday morning or sit behind a computer on a Monday, God wants to blend our vocation with our calling. Your vocation is special and your calling is sacred, regardless of whether you wear a clerical collar or a blue collar. No matter what job pays the bills at the end of the month, he wants you to come to terms with your calling and use your job to further his kingdom.

Down here we are an integral part of his kingdom. He gets the glory when we walk with him. One day we shall leave this world behind us when we enter his eternal kingdom and share his glory forever. What a day that will be!

This is what leadership is all about - it's giving people hope! Paul fulfilled that role admirably. He was a leader and a servant at the same time.

> *So let us learn how to serve,*
> *And in our lives enthrone him,*
> *Each other's needs to prefer,*
> *For it is Christ we're serving.*

CHAPTER 8

Faith - Family - Future

'And we also thank God continually because, when you received the word of God, which you heard from us, you accepted it not as the word of men, but as it actually is, the word of God, which is at work in you who believe. For you, brothers, became imitators of God's churches in Judea, which are in Christ Jesus: You suffered from your own countrymen the same things those churches suffered from the Jews, who killed the Lord Jesus and the prophets and also drove us out. They displease God and are hostile to all men in their effort to keep us from speaking to the Gentiles so that they may be saved. In this way they always heap up their sins to the limit. The wrath of God has come upon them at last. But, brothers, when we were torn away from you for a short time (in person, not in thought), out of our intense longing we made every effort to see you. For we wanted to come to you - certainly I, Paul, did, again and again - but Satan stopped us. For what is our hope, our joy, or the crown in which we will glory in the presence of our Lord Jesus Christ when he comes? Is it not you? Indeed, you are our glory and joy' (2:13-20)

Growing pains can be a problem! Perhaps that's an understatement! When you look at the final verses in chapter two there is ample evidence to suggest that the infant church in Thessalonica was going through something similar. They're stretching, they're developing, they're maturing, they're growing - and sometimes that can be painful. For them it certainly was. They faced many trials and much trouble. They suffered and their only crime was their sincere love for the Lord Jesus.

When you look objectively at their situation and analyse what is happening, one thing emerges - it was tough in the first century! Paul chose his words carefully as he summed up their predicament. He speaks of:

· *'severe suffering'* - that means pressure from circumstances,
· *'suffered'* - this is the same word that is used for the sufferings of Jesus,
· *'drove us out'* - means to be rejected by those to whom you seek to minister,
· *'hostile'* - used of winds that blow against us,
· *'stopped/hindered'* - pictures a road so broken that travel is impossible.

This was life as it really was. Life in the raw, life on the frontline. Remarkably though they still possessed a joy in their hearts (cf. 1:6). Paul, himself, was a worried man and deeply concerned about their welfare, yet he similarly displays a real joy in his life (cf. 2:19,20). The bottom line is that, no matter how adverse the circumstances, the Lord is always with us. He goes through it with us. We're not really on our own.

Paul shows them three resources which they have and on which they can depend when life is lived in a pressure cooker:

· we have the faith,
· we have the family,
· we have a future.

Paul thanks the Lord for them because of their attitude to the word of God. They accepted it not as the word of men, but as it is, the oracles of God. It is the living word of a God who is alive, a message that is unchanging, timeless, never dated. It speaks to the major issues of every generation. It holds the key to understanding the vital problems of our day. How did they see it?

They appreciated it!

They knew it was so much more than the words of mortal men. They passionately believed it to be the word of the Lord. The Bible is not like any other book. It stands alone and above all other books in the world. It's different. And, it's meant to be. It is different in origin, character and content. It is the word of God, inspired by the Spirit of God, for all the people of God. When we hear it or read it, we are receiving his message, listening to his voice, considering his thoughts.

They appropriated it!

There are two words Paul uses in verse 13 which shows their response to the ministry. The first is *'received'* and the second is *'accepted'*. The first term means *to accept it from another.* The second means *to welcome it warmly.* One has the idea of hearing with the ear; the other implies a hearing of the heart. They not only heard the word but they took it and made it part and parcel of their lives. They went through the word and the word went through them.

When Jesus was speaking to his followers he often directed their attention to their attitude to the word of his Father. In Matthew 13:9 the emphasis is, take heed *that* you hear. In Mark 4:24 the challenge is to take heed *what* you hear. Then in Luke 8:18 he exhorts them to take heed *how* you hear.

We need to learn the art of meditation, chewing the cud of Scripture. There's a lot to be said for quietly waiting upon the Lord as we ponder his word to our hearts. We should approach it with an intense longing to hear him speak. And, when he does, we should take time to let it sink in and soak our hearts. We will then become a people saturated with the word of God. The reality of Christ soaks into our lives so deeply and completely that it changes the very chemistry of our being.

They applied it!

They put it into practice. They were good listeners and they were good livers! They were doers of the word and from James 1:25 that's where the blessing is found. Therein lies the secret - living it out in the rough and tumble of daily life. At home, in college or university, in business, on the factory floor, wherever we are, it's all about living out the word of God. God's word changes people and, if you let it, it will change you too!

·   With the heart we appreciate it,
·   with the mind we appropriate it,
·   with the will we apply it.

It's the whole man controlled by all of the word so that we become men and women of the word. Isn't that exciting!

When trouble comes to our front door, how do we handle it? Sometimes we go down and under, sometimes we cave in and collapse under the pressure, sometimes we feel hurt and badly let down, sometimes when the enemy strikes we feel particularly vulnerable and isolated. At times we are prone to feel as though we are on our own and that we are the only ones going through a rough patch.

The abiding fact remains: we're not! Look at verses 14 and 15.

The harrowing experiences of those in Thessalonica was more or less a carbon copy of what was happening to those believers further east in Judea. There was nothing strange or sinister about their misfortune. In fact, it was to be expected. Sooner or later it was bound to happen. They would be stronger and better for it at the end of the day. They were only human, they had their feelings, but they were definitely not on their own!

Isn't that one of the great values of being part of the global family of God? We can stand together in our darkest hours. When the storm clouds gather we can cling to the Lord and hold on to one another. In the family of God we should be able to find in each other a measure of help and encouragement.

Remember our friend Elijah? It was when he isolated himself from the others that his heart sank to an all time low and he wanted to quit. Lonely saints are easy meat for the enemy. Whether we realise it or not, we need each other. We can't go it alone. In the battles of this life, together we can survive.

Paul wasn't ashamed to admit that he loved these dear people. They meant so much to him. In fact, he felt bereaved because he couldn't be with them. He felt as though he were an orphan (cf verse 17). He wanted to stay and minister to them but the enemy drove him out. He tried to return but, again, his path was blocked. There were obstacles strewn across the road and Satan effectively stopped him from making any headway.

How can we explain such an incident? It's all down to the overruling providence of the Lord. He can see tomorrow and we can only see today. Our disappointments are his appointments. God had something better - something around the bend he couldn't see.

So, what did he do? He didn't look back and give in to guilt feelings of regret and remorse. Rather, he looked forward, he looked ahead, and rejoiced. He scanned the horizon and saw his dear friends from Thessalonica in the presence of the Lord in glory. What a vision. It changed his outlook and gave him a brand new perspective on life in the here and now as he glimpsed the there and then!

Troubles will come, trials will come. There will be the inevitable growing pains. In such moments we need to take a long view of things. We need to view them from the vantage point of heaven. That's how Paul lived! He wanted to shape tomorrow so he started today. He planned not for the short term but for the long term. He had goals and went for them. His actions today were governed by what God may do tomorrow.

In spite of what some of them were saying about him in the church at Thessalonica, he knew that one day Christ would return and that the Lord would reward him. That's what kept him going. The real saints in the church would bring glory to the Lord and at the same time bring immense joy to his heart. They would become his crown of rejoicing, something he would gladly lay down at the feet of Jesus.

Such a prospect should spur us on. It should put the sparkle back into our lives. What a motivation! Jesus is coming. Oh yes, you'll have your ups and downs, you'll have your problems with people, you'll have many a hassle down here, but take heart, get excited, Christ is surely coming!

CHAPTER 9

Assurances about Affliction

'So when we could stand it no longer, we thought it best to be left by ourselves in Athens. We sent Timothy, who is our brother and God's fellow worker in spreading the gospel of Christ, to strengthen and encourage you in your faith, so that no-one would be unsettled by these trials. You know quite well that we were destined for them. In fact, when we were with you, we kept telling you that we would be persecuted. And it turned out that way, as you well know. For this reason, when I could stand it no longer, I sent to find out about your faith' (3:1-5a)

Warren Wiersbe in his excellent commentary on 1 Thessalonians has given us a succinct outline on the main thrust of the opening three chapters. He writes:

· in chapter 1 - how the church was born,
· in chapter 2 - how the church was nurtured,
· in chapter 3 - how the church was established.

It's all about finding our feet and learning to stand on them! We need to be grounded in the faith so that when the stormy winds of trial blow in our face we'll not fall flat. Consequently, he shows to us the path to spiritual maturity, the road down which we must go to obtain spiritual advancement.

The key word is found in verses 2 and 13. It is the word *'strengthen'*.

The key verse is verse 8 which reads: *'for now we really live, since you are standing firm in the Lord'.*

It's actually worthwhile noting that a little phrase appears five times in ten verses. He talks about *'your faith'.* That is both significant and suggestive:

·   in verse 2 it is the profession of your faith,
·   in verse 5 it is the examination of your faith,
·   in verse 6 it is the proclamation of your faith,
·   in verse 7 it is the consolation of your faith,
·   in verse 10 it refers to additions to your faith.

It's patently obvious from the opening verse that Paul's heart pined for them. He knew a measure of felt pain because he could not be with them. In fact it has become so bad he can't stand the strain any longer. The silence was unbearable and the suspense of wondering how things were going was proving too much for him to handle. He felt he couldn't sit back any more and worry any longer. He was frustrated. He found himself at breaking point and he longed for a measure of release and relief. Let's face it, he couldn't pick up the phone, he couldn't jump in the car and drive north, he couldn't send a fax or communicate by electronic mail. He was at wit's end corner and his back was to the wall.

He was in Athens and on the verge of going further south to Corinth but his heart was up north in Thessalonica. He knew where he preferred to be because they mean so much to him. They are his joy and crown. That explains why he feels overwhelmed with a sense of desolation. He feels abandoned. He feels deflated and all on his own. The implication behind his comments is that he is passing through something akin to a bereavement. In other words, part of him is missing.

So what does he do? Well, rather than go himself which would have been the easy option, he stays where he is, and he sends young Timothy on his behalf. He would be able to see them and enquire as to their spiritual health. He isn't overly concerned about their comfort, welfare or prosperity; it's their faith which he is most interested in. Surely that's symptomatic of a father's love for his children. What a man!

He couldn't have chosen anyone better than Timothy. He was a man after his own heart. Actually, he says of him in Philippians 2:20, *'I have no-one else like him, who takes a genuine interest in your welfare'.*

In one sense, he was Paul's trouble shooter, an emissary, a special agent. If something was broken in their fellowship, this young man would be the ideal man to fix it. We could say that he went there as a short term missionary. It's intriguing when you look at verse 2 and see how the older man describes the younger man. This little microchip description stores a world of information about his character. What a superb reference Paul gives him:

·   *'our brother'* - he was a saved man! They enjoyed a sweet relationship with each other. It was a joy and delight for Paul to have him as his right hand man;

·   *'God's fellow worker'* - he had a stable relationship with the Lord. We can see something here of the dignity of his role in life, he is God's, but he is also part of a team ministry in that they were fellows. He was a servant who was unafraid of hard work.

He had the sterling qualities which were needed to minister to young believers. He had patience and dedication combined with love and grace in his heart. He would become Paul's protege and one of the early church's first pastors.

What was his task?

It was twofold. Number one, it was to strengthen the believers as they were weak at the knees. The word means 'to shore up, to buttress'. They needed built up. Number two, it was to encourage the church because they were low in spirit. They needed a boost.

What was his goal?

The primary objective was so *'that no-one would be unsettled by these trials'.* He longs for them to stand firm and stand fast in the Lord. He has a fair idea what they are passing through and he is all too aware of the devastating consequences such difficult times can bring in their wake.

When we move into verses 3 and 4 we find him dealing there with the whole problem of affliction. He handles it as you would expect a man of his calibre to, both sensitively and sensibly. He is tactful and tender. He says three things about it:

He gives them an assurance!

Verse 4 tells me that affliction and trial is inevitable for the Christian. There is no getting away from it. The Christian life is not a Sunday School picnic nor one big spiritual Disneyland - it was never intended to be. It is not an easy alternative to life. Rather, trouble will come. Trials will come. And, they will hurt. We can't avoid them. They are an integral part of our experience. They are:

- our portion (Philippians 1:29)
- our privilege (Philippians 3:10)
- our power (2 Corinthians 12:9,10).

He talks about our attitude!

He says we were destined for them. They were coming our way, come what may! It's not the luck of the draw, it's not a matter of pulling the shortest straw. When trials come they are not accidents that just happen, they are by divine appointment. Nothing is happening to us by chance or coincidence - all is part of the outworking of God's plan for us. They are well within the scope of the will of God for our lives. The bottom line is that they can all be attributed to the providence of God. In such moments, we need to:

- recognise His purpose - there's always a lesson to be learned. Remember Joseph! They meant it for evil but God had other ideas. From the divine vantage point, it would be for his good and benefit. It's Romans 8:28 being activated as a powerful principle in our lives. Behind the dark threatening clouds the sun is still shining brightly;

- realise His perfection - David wrote after he was being hunted and hounded by his enemies that so far as he was concerned God's way was perfect;

- rest on His promise - when we compare Romans 8:18 everything is brought sharply into focus. The problems remain but they are only for a moment in the light of an eternity spent in the presence of the Lord. It may be traumatic down here but it can't be compared to the glory which will be ours when we reach the other side;

- rejoice in His provision - He knows how much we can take and he will send us no more than we can bear. He doesn't make the back for the burden, but he makes each burden to suit the back. To put it frankly, our trials are tailor made for us!

He makes an assessment!

The word Paul has used in verse 4 is the word *'persecuted'* which speaks of intense pain, crippling heartache, enduring hardness. It has the idea of being often found in perilous situations where the pressures are both from without and within. Yes, our comfort zone will get the squeeze! God isn't interested in watching our faith get torpedoed by trials - every test is designed by God to stretch our faith. The fact is, when real faith is stretched, it doesn't break and when it is pressed, it doesn't fail.

You may be knocked down, but you will never be knocked out! You will never be counted out on the canvas!

Perhaps the moving words written from the heart by Andrae Crouch sum it up best when he says:

> *I thank God for the mountains and*
> *I thank him for the valleys,*
> *I thank him for the storms he brought me through,*
> *For if I'd never had a problem -*
> *I wouldn't know that he could solve them,*
> *I'd never know what faith in God could do.*
>
> *Through it all, through it all,*
> *Oh, I've learned to trust in Jesus,*
> *I've learned to trust in God.*
> *Through it all, through it all,*
> *I've learned to depend upon his word.*

CHAPTER 10

Truth about the Tempter

'I was afraid that in some way the tempter might have tempted you and our efforts might have been useless. But Timothy has just now come to us from you and has brought good news about your faith and love. He has told us that you always have pleasant memories of us and that you long to see us, just as we also long to see you. Therefore, brothers, in all our distress and persecution we were encouraged about you because of your faith. For now we really live, since you are standing firm in the Lord. How can we thank God enough for you in return for all the joy we have in the presence of our God because of you?' (3:5b - 9)

The devil is alive and kicking! And, he has been for a very long time. If you have any doubts about it, ask the folks in Thessalonica. Day after day he made a nuisance of himself in their situation - no matter where they turned he never seemed to be too far away. He was ever loitering with intent. And his aim was to make them stumble. He was only happy when they were the epitome of misery.

God's policy with regard to the tempter is this:

·   his scope is God determined - he can go so far and no further,
·   his sphere is God defined - he can go so near and no closer,

·   his strength is God dictated - he can do so much and no more.

Rejoice! Because of Calvary, the tempter's power is broken.

What is his line of attack? How does he strike at you and me?
Paul has said elsewhere: *'I write so that Satan might not
outwit you, for we are not unaware of his schemes'*. It was Oscar
Wilde who quipped, 'I can resist everything except temptation'. It is
the oldest of all the inner conflicts in the heart of man. It stalks us all.

He wasn't the only one who had to cope with that particular
weakness as the same was true of Mark Antony. He was known as
the silver throated orator of Rome. He was also credited with being
a brilliant man, a strong leader, and a courageous soldier. The one
thing he lacked was strength of character. On the outside he was
powerful and impressive - on the inside he was weak and vulnerable.
His tutor is reputed to have been so enraged on one occasion that he
shouted at him, 'O Marcus! O colossal child ... able to conquer the
world but unable to resist a temptation'. We know the sequel to the
story for his most widely known and costly temptation sailed up the
river to him on a barge. Cleopatra captured his unguarded heart.
Their sinful relationship cost him his wife, his place as a world
leader, and ultimately his life.

He may surprise us!

Remember the classic example of David and Bathsheba. It was the
most unlikely moment. He was caught napping, his guard was down.
He was torn apart in a moment of time when he was least expecting
it. It only took a split second for him to court spiritual disaster.

He may use the siege method!

His intent is clear from Daniel 7 where we are reminded that *'he shall wear out the saints'.* Constant pressure can crack us. We break up, then break down, and he breaks in! He will tell you that your circumstances are far too difficult, that your past failures have weakened you too much. He will highlight our inability to overcome some besetting sin. His tactics are to wear us down until we can take no more. He knows our weakest point. He can always locate the chink in the armour.

He may be subtle!

He's the master of disguise. When he approaches us as an angel of light he makes sin look innocent. Remember Adam and Eve. Instead of food they found poison, instead of satisfaction they found shame, instead of pleasure they found pain. In Matthew 4 he tried to trip up the Lord Jesus by adopting similar tactics. We know the sequel - he was unsuccessful!

Now you can see why Paul promptly despatched young Timothy as his special envoy. It all fits neatly into place. It all comes together and makes sense. When you turn to verse 6 he has returned and his important assignment has been ably carried out. He has done the job Paul asked him to do and the news is good news.

That phrase *'good news'* is the same as we use when we speak of the gospel. It is glad tidings. When Paul heard Timothy's glowing report he felt as if he was being saved all over again. He's like a new man. He's ecstatic, jubilant and rejuvenated. This was the morale booster he desperately required. It was like a tonic to his soul, it really thrilled him. It was comparable to a refreshing spring shower.

It's hard to believe, isn't it. But Paul was made of the same material as the rest of us. He's no different to you and me. Sadly, we elevate these men into super saints when the fact of the matter is they are made of exactly the same stuff as we are. We put them on a pedestal when in reality their feet are standing on the same old world as yours and mine. Paul was having an 'off day' - he was on a real downer. He was depressed, disheartened and discouraged. His outlook changed, however, when he heard the brilliant news from Timothy. It did the trick. His battery was recharged, it set the adrenaline flowing in his veins, he got a second wind. Now, he's back to his usual good self. To Paul, in the middle of his arid wasteland of loneliness, Timothy's report was a lush oasis of hope.

Timothy has talked about their faith and their love and given a clear indication that they were really going on with the Lord. They were reaching out to others. In many areas, they were lengthening the cords and strengthening the stakes. They were hyperactive in the work of God. They were truly on the ball. On a spiritual level, they were alive and well. They were standing firm against the world's erosion.

They had pleasant memories of Paul and his short visit with them. That meant so much to Paul because at this point he was feeling rejected and dejected. He had often wondered in his heart, was it really worth it? He felt as though he was past his sell-by date. His mind was working overtime and so many issues were being blown out of all perspective. The longer he wallowed in his despair the more introverted and self conscious he became. He felt as if he had blown it and that he was just a wretched failure who was coming apart at the seams. Now, Timothy reassures him that they remember him with fond affection and they likewise had hoped that their paths would cross again. Whether we're a Paul or not, we all need to feel accepted and we all need to feel as though our ministry is being appreciated. Sometimes we're inclined to forget that the best of men are only men at best.

What impact did this all have on the apostle? It was like a bridge in that it helped him to reach the other side. According to verse 7 he is enormously encouraged. He talks about his distress which means the kind of trouble that has a crushing effect on you. He speaks of his persecution which means the kind of pressure that has a choking effect on you. He was left breathless as it were. He felt stifled. But this was the best news he could have possibly heard.

Why did he feel the way he did? Well, he's at Athens, and he's on his own! He had one experience after another of apparent defeat since he set foot in Europe. Yes, he responded to the call, *'come over and help us'*. And he went. He got more than he bargained for in that it was one trial after another. Any clear thinking man would automatically question all of this in his own mind. He could be forgiven for asking himself, 'Did I get it wrong?'

·   at Philippi he had been thrown into jail and asked to leave the city,
·   at Thessalonica he had been forced to leave and also give a guarantee that he wouldn't return,
·   at Berea he was hounded by Jews and compelled to move on,
·   at Athens he has seen little success with the philosophers of the city.

So this news from Timothy was just what he needed. His life was wrapped up in theirs in that he was one with them. This is body ministry, pure and simple. Because of this he is able to break forth into a paean of praise in verse 9. He says a sincere thankyou to the Lord for them. They mean more to him than words can tell. He's lost for words when he thinks about them in prayer. *'How can we thank God enough for you?'* That's the kind of relationship, the kind of bond, we should all be pursuing. When we meet each other, wouldn't it be wonderful to say: 'Thank you Lord for he's my brother, she's my sister'. It's not a back slapping service nor is it a mutual admiration society. It's a realisation that since we belong to the Lord we really do belong to each other.

> *Bind us together Lord*
> *bind us together*
> *with cords that cannot be broken.*
> *Bind us together Lord*
> *bind us together*
> *Oh, bind us together with love.*

CHAPTER 11

A Benediction of Blessing

'Night and day we pray most earnestly that we may see you again and supply what is lacking in your faith. Now may our God and Father himself and our Lord Jesus clear the way for us to come to you. May the Lord make your love increase and overflow for each other and for everyone else, just as ours does for you. May he strengthen your hearts so that you will be blameless and holy in the presence of our God and Father when our Lord Jesus Christ comes with all his holy ones' (3:10-13)

The young church at Thessalonica was upmarket and 'user friendly. They were aware of and alive to the needs of their generation. They were scratching where people were itching and because of their effervescent testimony were answering the questions people were asking. It could be rightly said of them that they were geared to their times and at all times they were anchored to the word. They stayed up with their times without looking down on the word.

Paul has been showing us in chapter 3 how the church was established - they were rooted and grounded in the word of God. There were no gimmicks, no instant formula to spiritual success, just the word of God. Paul had taught them well, Timothy made a worthwhile contribution, and between them they gave the church a solid foundation. They were anchored to the word. That gave them a good start in their Christian life, it gave them a springboard to reach new heights in their quest for the Lord.

Paul's letter is saturated with Bible teaching - every major doctrine is covered to a greater or lesser degree. From their perspective, doctrine was not dry and dull, it was dynamic. It was their life blood. Exciting!

What has Paul done for them? He has sent them a special envoy in Timothy, he has written a letter to them, now he says a prayer on their behalf. It's a three-fold prayer:

·   that their faith might mature (verse 10)
·   that their love may abound (verse 12)
·   that their lives might be holy (verse 13).

He wants to see them again. That's the deep longing of his heart as there was a refreshing spontaneity about their relationship. They always brought a smile to his face. They were number one on his priority list. He was so serious about prayer that he intercedes for them night and day. That's how much the church meant to him. His passion for them is that they might grow in grace and go on with the Lord. He wants them to make spiritual headway, to progress, to develop. There's no point in them back pedalling. And, there's certainly no mileage to be gained by standing still.

Faith is like a muscle - you either use it or lose it. It's equally true to say, the more you use it the stronger it becomes. It must be exercised or it will atrophy. The obvious example of that principle is Abraham:

- he believed God when he knew not where he was going
  (Hebrews 11:8)
- he believed God when he knew not how it would happen
  (Hebrews 11:11)
- he believed God when he knew not why God led him the way he
  did (Hebrews 11:17-19).

Oh yes, God will test our faith, not to destroy it, but to develop it. A faith that cannot be tested cannot be trusted!

That was what Paul prayed. Imagine his joy when a short time later he writes them another letter and he's able to say that God answered his prayer. We read in 2 Thessalonians 1:3, *'We thank God for you ... because your faith is growing more and more'*.

His conclusion!

Verse 11 is a moving reminder to us that Paul has come to the end of himself. He is aware of his inadequacy and inability. He knows that even though he can't do it, God can. Is anything too hard for the Lord? He puts the ball back into God's court for he is the master of the situation. He is able to solve the crisis. He can undo the tangled mess. It's a well thought out decision on his part to say: 'It's over to him!'

His consolation!

He knew in his heart of hearts that only God could open up the way ahead. The path was strewn with many obstacles, it was lined with many hindrances. On a human level, it was impossible. But it is in such situations where God delights to prove his ability - he specialises in such situations. He is the God who has come from somewhere, and he is the God who can get you where you're going.

His challenge!

He is resigned to the will of God. He knows that God's way is always the best way. For him there is no viable alternative - anything else would be unthinkable. It may not be the easiest path to go down, but it is always the preferred option. He reckons it is better to be alone with God than it is to be in the crowd without him. God is bigger than all our problems. There's no hill too high for him, no valley too low for him. He is the God of all our tears and fears.

Operation Agape is launched in verse 12 when Paul's prayer shows his all consuming desire for them is that their love may abound. This is getting your hands dirty in the service of Jesus. It's getting your feet wet in ministering to others in his name.

In the context of what Paul is saying here we need to remember that suffering is never far from his mind. Suffering isn't the only problem - it's how we handle it when it comes knocking at the front door of our lives. Sometimes our times of suffering can turn into times of selfishness. We can so quickly become insular, parochial and self-centred. We can be so demanding on those around us - we can be hard to live with when everything in the garden doesn't appear to be overly rosy.

What life does to us depends on what life finds in us. Nothing reveals the true heart of man like the furnace of affliction. Trials will bring out the best in you - they can also bring out the worst. It depends on how we react and respond.

When the going gets tough some people will build a wall. They will shut themselves in and cut themselves off from others. Other people, however, will build a bridge enabling them to reach out to others. When they do that they are brought closer to the Lord and to his people.

Did you really notice what Paul prayed? It is that *'their love may increase and overflow for each other'*. Wonder of wonders, his prayer was answered! Read all about it in 2 Thessalonians 1:3 where Paul writes: *'the love every one of you has for each other is increasing'*.

Yes, it was Paul's request that their love might be full and overflowing - a love for one another - a love for those outside the family of God - the unloved and the unlovable - the unlikely candidates - none should feel unloved. We can love them all through Jesus. Actually, it's a command to be obeyed. This was the badge worn on the lapel of their lives. They wore their religion on their sleeve. The mark of a healthy church is when others are able to say: *'see how they love each other'*.

Abounding love must never be bound. It's always reaching out. It expands. It is all embracing. Love always looks after number two - not exclusively after number one. It goes beyond the call and claim of duty. It goes far beyond the suggested second mile. When you share and show love to other people in an unconditional and unselfish manner, you always walk away the winner. Not only are others enriched, so are you! Of course, when you love this way, you become vulnerable. But if you never step out on a limb with people and take a risk, you'll never grasp the fruit of nourishing relationships. In the final analysis, it is God touching men through ordinary people like you and me.

Here was a church where faith was vibrant, a fellowship pulsating with life and a place where love was warmly felt. An exciting church? It's got to be!

His final request and petition is that their lives might be holy. Again, this is linked to the soon return of our Lord. It's the advent of Jesus that is brought sharply into focus. That's what puts everything into proper perspective. He longs that when they stand before the Lord they will be:

- *'blameless'* - i.e. with no blemishes on their lives,
- *'holy'* - i.e. with no blots on their character.

He is pointing forward to the day he referred to in 2 Corinthians 5:10 when we will be called to give an account of the service we have rendered to the Lord. It's a personal encounter and interview with Jesus. Paul is reminding them that they are responsible down here for they will be accountable up there!

He wants to be able to present us as a pure virgin to Christ (2 Corinthians 11:2), he wants his bride to be a glorious church, a radiant church, without stain or wrinkle or any other blemish (cf. Ephesians 5:27). Stains are caused by defilement on the outside and blemishes are caused by decay on the inside.

Today's church is not perfect! But then:

> *When he shall come with trumpet sound,*
> *O may I then in him be found;*
> *Dressed in his righteousness alone -*
> *Faultless to stand before the throne.*

For us to be acceptable there, we must be accepted here. When you go back to the word you will discover there are three grounds of our acceptance. There is:

- the Beloved in whom we are accepted (Ephesians 1:6)
- the belief through which we are accepted (1 Timothy 1:15)
- the behaviour by which we are accepted (2 Corinthians 5:9).

One day, one glorious morning, Paul's prayer will be finally answered, for we know that, *'when he shall appear, we shall be like him, for we shall see him as he is'.*

I believe that is the essence of an exciting church! It's getting on with the job down here, it's standing up and being counted for God, it's facing trials and winning the battle, it's being strong and stable in our personal commitment to Jesus, it's having an eye for eternity for the countdown to his coming is getting lower every day.

The outcome is inevitable - our faith will mature, our love will abound and our lives will be holy. That means, we will be geared to the times and anchored to the word.

- Let's grow wiser!
- Let's grow stronger!
- Let's grow purer!

CHAPTER 12

Helps to Holiness

'Finally, brothers, we instructed you how to live in order to please God, as in fact you are living. Now we ask you and urge you in the Lord Jesus to do this more and more. You know what instructions we gave you by the authority of the Lord Jesus. It is God's will that you should be holy' (4:1-3a)

Have you heard the latest definition of an optimist? It's someone who believes the preacher is almost finished when he says 'finally'. That's choice, isn't it.

Did you see the opening word in chapter 4? You've guessed it! It's the word *finally*. The interesting thing from a statistics point of view is that in chapters 1-3 there is a total of 43 verses, when you count up chapters 4 and 5 there are 46 verses. So, what does Paul mean when he says *finally?*

It's almost like a change of gear, he's moving into overdrive. It's the punchline. He has given them a crash course in Bible doctrine in chapters 1-3; in the following two chapters he is encouraging them to let the rubber hit the road. They have learned all about it - now they needed to go and live it out and prove that it really works. That's where doctrine is gripping stuff.

The bottom line in your life and mine is that we should be walking with the Lord. In fact, that's the picture often painted in the Word of God. We are to *'walk worthy of the vocation wherewith we have been called ... walk in love ... walk as children of light'*. Why a walk?

· It demands life, for a dead sinner cannot walk
· it requires growth, for a little baby cannot walk
· it requires liberty, for someone who is bound cannot walk
· it demands light, for no one wants to walk in the dark
· it cannot be hidden, for it is witnessed by all
· it suggests progress towards a goal.

The Christian life begins with a step of faith and that single step should lead to a life of walking by faith. *'For we walk by faith, not by sight'*. That's not a step into the dark, it's a leap forward into the light.

Have you ever wondered how we should be walking? Paul leaves us in no doubt, for we read in chapter 4.

· we are to walk in holiness (verses 1-8)
· we are to walk in harmony (verses 9,10)
· we are to walk in honesty (verses 11,12)
· we are to walk in hope (verses 13-18).

Paul is telling the church in these opening verses what God expects of each of us. He reminds us of the will of God for our lives. Holiness of life is the standard he has set down. Then, he pulls the carpet from under our feet and says in verses 3 to 8 that we *'should avoid sexual immorality'*. He's talking here to Christians. Like us, they were living in a moral fog, and so he gives them some straight talk on moral purity. He deals with the problem of handling the sex drive within each of us. He feels very strongly that it all starts with a clear perception of holiness in our lives.

You can see the standard Paul has set by his comments in verse 1. He wants them to live a life that is pleasing to the Lord. That is a path of implicit obedience to the word of God. It is when we walk in the ways of the Lord and when we are totally abandoned to his will.

Remember Enoch. He had an outstanding testimony in that it is said of him, *'he pleased God'*. Sometimes, human nature being what it is, we try to please ourselves. Maybe we fall into the trap of attempting to please other people. What really matters more than anything else is that we always seek to please the Lord. Paul could write elsewhere: *'for if I yet pleased men, I should not be the servant of Christ'* and *'even so we speak, not as pleasing men, but God'*.

The inescapable fact is that he who tries to please everybody ends up pleasing nobody.

So, how do we please the Lord? By doing the will of God!

Sanctification is God's will for our lives. However, the minute you mention such a subject people are often confused. They have a pot pourri of weird and wonderful ideas as to what it is and what it isn't. Some think of it as a kind of religious sheep dip they are put through, a once for all experience of cleansing and commitment. Once they have been dipped, they think everything is fine. Others see sanctification as an extraction process whereby God uses a kind of supernatural magnet to remove all sin from our lives, and from that moment on they argue they will have no trouble pleasing him.

If the truth be told, the word 'sanctification' is almost the same as the word 'holiness' in that they both come from the same root. Sadly, holiness hasn't had a particularly good press in recent times. It's often a non-starter with the average person. People are turned off by it. They see so-called holy people as those who have been soaked in embalming fluid. They are dour and dull and have the knack of frowning on anything that smacks of fun or pleasure. Christians are not meant to have a good time or enjoy a good laugh, according to them that is not holiness.

The Old Testament speaks about *'the beauty of holiness'* in that there is a loveliness associated with it. There is something attractive about a life lived the way God intended. This means that God is designing beautiful people, not merely on the outside, but those who are beautiful on the inside. People who are admirable, trustworthy, strong, loving, compassionate - people who are whole. That is, people who are holy - they are sanctified.

We're the religion of the clean life and pure heart. That's something positive. It means we are monopolised by him, we cleave and cling to him, we are exclusively for the Master's use. It is when we turn our back on sin and on sensual pleasures, when we leave the world behind us, when we burn all our bridges. You can't have anything more meaningful than that. Here is the key that unlocks the door to a deeper spiritual life. It will lead us to a new dimension of Christian living. It will enable us to scale new heights with the Lord. Here is life on a higher plane - a sanctified life.

It means we are set apart by him, for him, and to him. Even after God has declared us righteous, his next step is to make us righteous. That's what sanctification is all about!

This is the picture you have in the heart of the Old Testament. There we read that the Sabbath was sanctified as a day of rest, the Tabernacle and Temple were sanctified as they were set apart by

God's presence, God sanctified the nation of Israel as his own possession, he sanctified the sons of Levi to serve in his courts in a priestly ministry - it just means: they were set apart by him and for him.

In many ways, it is similar to our salvation in that it is in three tenses. We can say, we have been saved, we are being saved, and we will be saved.

We can also declare:

· we have been sanctified - that's in the past
· we are being sanctified - that's in the present
· we will be sanctified - that's prospective.

Yesterday ...

I was set apart from the penalty of sin. That is something positional in nature. It is what happened at the moment of my conversion.

Today ...

I am being set apart from the power of sin. That is something progressive in that it is an ongoing and daily experience. It is gradual.

Tomorrow ...

I will be set apart from the presence of sin. That is something perpetual for we read in 1 John 3:3, *'How great is the love the Father has lavished on us that we should be called children of God. Dear friends, now we are children of God, and we know that when he appears we shall be like him for we shall see him as he is'.*

- We can look back and say, Christ for me!
- We can reflect on the present and say, Christ in me!
- We can look forward with anticipation and say, Christ with me!

The ethos and heartbeat of sanctification is that the Lord has set apart him that is godly for himself. With that in mind, it is interesting to discover that the Trinity plays a part in our sanctification. Jude reminds us that the Father decrees it in that it is his purpose and plan. Hebrews tells us that the Son determines it because this is one of the benefits of the atonement. Romans indicates that the Spirit directs it through the application of the word of God. A similar note is struck in John 17:17,19 where the Saviour prayed: *'Sanctify them by the truth. Your word is truth'.*

The word of God is the agent of sanctification. As we read the word and hear it ministered it will have a cleansing effect on our lives. It will meet our needs. It will show up the spots and stains. It will reveal the blemishes. We will see ourselves as God sees us. Then as we allow the water of the word to wash us, to purify us, we will become more holy. We become more like Jesus.

This great ministry of sanctification implies:

- a cleansing - he is looking for clean vessels and the only way to do that is to mortify the old nature and feed the new man,
- a commissioning - we are vessels designed for service. We are sanctified so that he might send us into a lost world with the message of redeeming love. We should be practising our position in Christ,
- a Christ-likeness - we should be holy within and without like Jesus.

This, according to Paul, is the will of God for each of our lives. We are sanctified, therefore, we should live like saints. Saints are not those who have been canonised but those who have been called and cleansed. They are not those set in stained glass, but those living in today's world in a pagan culture.

It's a matter for the heart, and the heart of the matter is our personal holiness. That was ever the supreme concern of Robert Murray McCheyne who often said, 'My people's greatest need is my personal holiness'.

CHAPTER 13

Maintaining Moral Purity

'You should avoid sexual immorality; that each of you should learn to control his own body in a way that is holy and honourable, not in passionate lust like the heathen, who do not know God; and that in this matter no-one should wrong his brother or take advantage of him. The Lord will punish men for all such sins, as we have already told you and warned you. For God did not call us to be impure, but to live a holy life. Therefore, he who rejects this instruction does not reject man but God, who gives you his Holy Spirit' (4:3b-8)

These first generation believers in Thessalonica were living on the cutting edge of their society. To them, Paul explains the ethos of having a faith that is exciting. It is based on the premise of a life that is pleasing to the Lord. This will be seen in many different areas but here in this section he singles out one particular aspect for special attention. He addresses the subject of our relationship with members of the opposite sex. He handles it tenderly and tactfully. At the same time, however, there is a toughness in his approach when he reminds them of the consequences of disobeying the word of God. He deals sensitively with the subject of sex. It is straight talk about moral purity. Charles Swindoll aptly comments, 'here we have grass stained advice from someone following Christ in the grass roots of life.'

I suppose these words are rarely preached upon. They're not very high on the popularity ratings for selecting as your favourite portion of the word of God. And yet, how exceedingly relevant they are in our post-Christian era.

We live in a grossly immoral society where anything goes. The standards of acceptable behaviour have plummeted to an all-time low. We are on a downward spiral and teetering on the brink of disaster. I believe we have gone full circle. We are living dangerously as we have returned to the days of Noah and Lot. So many vital issues are blurred in the moral fog which is so prevalent at this moment. This is an hour of enormous need, and the great need of the hour is for the people of God to maintain moral purity. Paul here is gutsy, honest and sincere to the core as he probes into the nerve centre of our lives. He's right on target as he pinpoints the very things that need our immediate attention. It has been said that 'the practice of purity causes us to stand out from the world like a diamond against black velvet.'

We are saints, we are sanctified, we are called to live separated lives unto the Lord, we are told to be different from the world, we are exhorted to be a holy people. That means, in the context of these few verses, that God is looking for a people who will be sanctified through and through - he wants purity of life, purity of heart, and purity of mind.

He is looking for young people who will flee youthful lusts. He is looking for middle aged folks who will show by their lifestyle and behaviour that God's way is the best way. He's looking for older folks who will set an example of godliness, of what it really means to have a clean heart. What a tremendous challenge!

The purpose!

Did you see what Paul is saying? In one breath he declares, 'It is

God's will that you should be sanctified' and in the next breath he says, 'that you should avoid sexual immorality'. Sanctification affects every department of our lives. Paul's teaching here is plain, clear and distinct. He tells it like it is.

The Christian should have nothing to do with that which is labelled immoral in our minds, in our hearts, with our eyes, and with our bodies. He says we should avoid it like the plague. It's not just the act - it's the attitude as well. Don't play with fire or you'll get badly burned. Let me spell it out clearly:

- immorality means no sexual wrongdoing,
- it means no fooling around in the back of a car,
- it means no premarital sex,
- it means no messing around with someone else's partner,
- it means no homosexual relationships,
- it means no pornography either in books, glossy magazines, TV or whatever.

Paul says: 'Have none of these things going on in your life'.

J. B. Phillips translates verse 3 with: *'God's plan is to make you holy, and that entails first of all, a clean break with sexual immorality'.*

The privilege!

We should be in charge of our own bodies and when we are God will be glorified. This is something we have to learn as it doesn't come naturally or easily. It's a lesson we must learn if we are to grow spiritually and if our lives are to count for God. We need to gain the mastery over our bodies so that we will not be a slave to them. We need to know victory over the flesh. We need to see the enemy running when he would seek to seduce us and try to tempt us.

It's a battle. The conflict is internal. The world is against us. The flesh is easy meat for the devil. That's the reason behind the Pauline injunction to control it! He's talking here about self discipline for purity is a conscious choice, it doesn't just happen.

The peril!

We are encouraged to look at the activities of the heathen around us and see how the sinner operates. Their lives are governed by lust, they are controlled by their passions, they are ruled by sensual desire and live according to the dictates and demands of the flesh. Basically, they do not know the Lord.

Paul reckons we should be different for we know the Lord Jesus. Our God is a reality in our lives. Therefore, in terms of moral behaviour, we should be an example. We should be setting the tone of every conversation. We should be seen to be above reproach in the community. We should exercise care and caution in the programmes we watch on television. We need to be selective in what we allow our eyes to focus and feast upon. That inevitably means some of the material on our screens and newsprint will be out of bounds for the person who is sensitive to the Spirit of God. If we tantalise ourselves with sin we end up morally weakened.

That means, from verse 5, we should not ignore the warning lights. When the red light is flashing we should be extra careful. Because of who we are in Christ we should be a good example to those around us.

The prohibition!

Paul really lays it on the line as to what is on the mind and heart of God. When a man commits fornication or engages in adultery it has a two fold effect. Firstly, he does wrong in that he oversteps the mark. He goes too far and transgresses. Secondly, he takes advantage of the other person. He is guilty of fraud. He wants something and goes for something that isn't his. He is covetous and falls foul to the avarice and selfish greed of his heart.

That's strong language. And yet when you sit down and hear what God is saying, we know it's true and we know it makes a lot of sense.

He uses the word *'brother'* here in verse 6 which in itself is most illuminating. This is the only time he uses this particular word as it means not only a brother in the Christian family but also includes our fellow man. The implication is that this kind of behaviour can never be acceptable. It is never viewed as the norm in the eyes of the Lord. Because of that we can never justify it either.

What are the consequences? *'The Lord will punish men for all such sins'.* There is coming a day of accountability, a day of reckoning, a day when all will be revealed. God sees all, he knows all, and all impurity he will judge.

If you fall, if you stray, if you do it, there is forgiveness with the Lord if you genuinely seek him in repentance. Yes, he will forgive your sin, but you will have to live with the repercussions of such a step for the rest of your life. The scars will remain. That's why in matters of leadership in the local church, Paul writes to Timothy and declares that such men should be *'the husband of one wife'* - that does not only mean he is married to one woman, but that he is a one-woman man!

Sin is sin! Someone criticised their pastor on one occasion for preaching against sin in the life of the Christian. They felt that sin in the life of a believer was different from sin in the life of an unconverted person. The pastor thought for a few moments and then he said: "Yes, you're right, it's worse!" God will never condemn sin in the sinner and condone it in the lives of his children.

The perspective!

God has called us to a life of holiness - a life of wholeness. He wants us to move out of the fog of impurity and into the bright light of holiness. That's why he has saved us, redeemed us, chosen us and cleansed us - the goal is that we might be a holy people.

The profession!

A close reading of verse 8 indicates that there are three steps to a life of holiness. We need to:

· recognise his presence - we have been given the Spirit of God and he abides within,
· respect his person - he is the *'Holy'* Spirit,
· receive his power - he alone can make us holy.

The choice is ours! Do we live horizontally in the weakness of the flesh or do we live vertically in the dynamic and power of the Spirit? A holy man is an awesome weapon in the hand of God. Paul is making a plea for purity so that we might be enabled by him to go out and live for Jesus in a world that is rotten to the core. One commentator has said: 'Purity involves more than a passing glance to see how much dirt we have under our finger nails. It requires a good, soaped-up, scrubbed-down Saturday night bath.'

What a challenge! A daunting task, it certainly is! It's still exciting, though!

CHAPTER 14

Reaching for the Stars

'Now about brotherly love we do not need to write to you, for you yourselves have been taught by God to love each other. And in fact, you do love all the brothers throughout Macedonia. Yet we urge you, brothers, to do so more and more. Make it your ambition to lead a quiet life, to mind your own business and to work with your hands, just as we told you, so that your daily life may win the respect of outsiders and so that you will not be dependent on anybody' (4:9-12)

William Cowper was prolific with the pen. Many of his hymns we love to sing as they mean so much to us. He writes from his heart. What he composed was often born in personal experience. He was the son of a local vicar who was the chaplain to King George II. His mother died when he was only six years of age. His father packed him off to a boarding school where he was often bullied and beaten. He was the object of fun and derision among his peers. His childhood and teenage years were full of loneliness, fear and insecurity.

Eventually he embarked on a career in law being called to the Bar. He practised there for a few years after which he was nominated for a position of eminence in the House of Lords. That was something he couldn't handle. It got too much for him and resulted in an attempted suicide. For two years he was confined to an asylum - all this before he was 30 years old.

He came out of the hospital and had more than his fair share of ups and downs. He moved across to Olney in Buckinghamshire to be close to John Newton. They had a superbly happy fellowship with each other but Cowper was often immersed in dark clouds of depression and despair. He was frequently plunged into long bouts of deep darkness. It was in many of these bad spells that he put pen to paper and wrote some of his best loved hymns. It was at such a moment that he penned the words: *God moves in a mysterious way, his wonders to perform.*

He wasn't always on a downer, though. There were many days when sunshine filled his heart. There were some pleasant hours when he lived on the top of the mountain. By contrast, it was on one of those occasions when he penned the hymn that has been impacting my heart in preparation for this chapter:

O for a closer walk with God, a calm and heavenly frame,
A light to shine upon the road, that leads me to the Lamb.

How many times we have echoed those sentiments!

Paul felt exactly the same for that's the thread woven into the fabric of chapter 4 of his letter to the infant church in Thessalonica. He longs that they might walk closely with the Lord and seek in all that they do to please him. How can that be achieved? According to verses 1-8 we are encouraged to walk in holiness as this is the will of God for us. We are a sanctified people and in the context of what Paul is teaching it means we are to aspire after moral purity. He has shown us how to conduct ourselves in a sex mad society.

In verses 9-12 he outlines two further aspects of our walk with the Lord. He says in verses 9 and 10 that we are to walk in harmony; and, in verses 11 and 12 we are to walk in honesty.

You can almost feel the change of atmosphere in verse 9 as there is a different tone here. He says, *'Now, I want to talk about brotherly love'*. Again, this should be the hallmark of the Christian. We should be known for our love for one another. He wants us to abound in affection.

An explanation of love!

The brand of love that Paul is talking about here is *philadelphia* love. It's the love that binds our hearts together. We're the children of God, we are brothers and sisters in the family of God, he is our Father, and he is love! In other words, the more we live like God in a life of purity, the more we will love one another. It's a love of deep affection that brings us out of our ivory theological towers to get involved in helping others in the trenches of life.

They were *'taught by God'* which seems quite remarkable. That's how they were able to do it. It was the work of God in their hearts. It was an operation of the Spirit deep within.

·   It's a family love - we have kindred hearts and minds as we have something in common. The ground was level at Calvary. It was said of those in the first century: *'see how they love each other'*.

·   It's a fragrant love - when there is love shared among us there will be a richness and a wonder in the atmosphere. You can tell if people love one another.

·   It's a fruitful love - we will want the best for each other, we will not rest until we see Christ shining from one another's lives, we will seek to discern the glory of God in all that we do together in his name.

The extent of love!

How much are we to love one another?

God the Father taught us to love each other when he gave Christ to die for us - we love him because he first loved us. God the Son taught us to love each other when he said: *'A new commandment I give unto you, that ye love one another'.* God the Holy Spirit taught us to love each other when he poured out the love of God in our hearts when we trusted Christ.

We are to show that kind of love to all the brethren and there are no exceptions. None are to be left out or excluded in any way. That's not easy sometimes. It goes against the grain at other times. For it is true:

> *To dwell above with saints in love*
> *That will indeed be glory.*
> *To dwell below with saints we know,*
> *Well, that's another story!*

Sometimes we hurt each other by the comments that we make, by the things that we do. Or, perhaps don't say or do! There are just some people who are easy to get along with and there are others who rub you up the wrong way. They tramp on your toes! We all have our own ideas, we will always have our differences of opinion, we all have our peculiarities, it's just that some are more eccentric than others. But, says Paul, we can still love each other. That's where love wins the day. That's where love overcomes the problems. That's where love goes beyond the clash of personalities. That's where love accepts the other person for who they are. That's where love always finds a way.

The expression of love!

Their love was known throughout Macedonia. How would they do it? It appears that one of the most obvious ways was through the ministry of hospitality. Open hearts and open homes. Love is the hinge on which hospitality turns to open its door.

From Hebrews 13 we are exhorted to show hospitality to three kinds of people - to saints, to strangers, and to those who are suffering.

Paul was all too aware that they were loving many different types of people but he urged them to keep it up. They were not to mark time or even maintain the status quo. He wants them to go out and break new ground for the Lord, to expand their love, to reach out more and more. The bottom line is that you can never get too much love and you can never give too much love!

And, his prayer was answered. See what he says in 2 Thessalonians 1:3b.

Now, having given them a lecture on love, he moves on to give them some instructions on integrity. It's all about walking in honesty. The opening phrase of verse 11 is an encouragement and incentive to them to be ambitious. There's nothing wrong with healthy ambition. It all depends what it is focused upon. Is it popularity, power, position or prestige? If it is, we're barking up the wrong tree!

Paul uses the same word three times in the New Testament. In Romans 15:20 it was his all consuming passion to reach the unreached with the message of Jesus and his love. He wanted to tell the gospel to the untold millions. Again, we come across it in 2 Corinthians 5:9 where his sincerely held desire is that in everything he might please the Lord Jesus. The third occasion is right here in our chapter. It is a three fold ambition:

· *'to lead a quiet life'*
· *'to mind your own business'*
· *'to work with your hands'.*

What does he mean by each of these?

Don't irritate!

To lead a quiet life means to be tranquil on the inside. It's not what you see advertised in the tabloid press when they encourage you to pay a visit to the local health shop to buy a bottle of tablets designed to give you perfect peace. It's not the hermit mentality either. No, it's living on the ragged edge with a peace in your heart and mind. It is contentment. It is when you feel relaxed in his love as you rest in his care. It's all about learning to lean on the Lord. This rich quality is found as we wait upon the Lord.

Don't interfere!

Paul pulls no punches when he bluntly tells them not to meddle in other people's affairs. They are to keep their own nose clean and not barge into other situations unless they are first invited. They must not gatecrash into someone else's privacy. As one translation declares: *don't be a busybody.* I'm sure this applies to every aspect of life - in the church, in the local community, in business, and certainly in the family!

Don't idle!

He is reminding them that there is no virtue in living like a parasite. If you have a job to do, thank God for it, and get on and do it. Don't be a time waster. Use every moment God has allocated to you and invest it wisely for him. Sleepers are an asset, but only on a railway line! Why bother working? The devil finds work for idle hands to do!   It was Mark Twain who said: 'I do not like work even when someone else does it.'

Honesty is not the best policy for the Christian, it's the only one! That's supremely the reason why we need to be men and women of ambition.

There's another angle to view it from, as the world is watching. The unconverted are looking at our lives. They see us, they know us. Paul reminds us if we are the kind of people God wants us to be then they will respect us for who and what we are. We will bear a good testimony. Others will look and we don't want them to point a finger as we should be above reproach.

Remember Enoch, that's how he operated. He walked with God, he pleased God, and when he was gone to glory, he was missed!

What a stimulating challenge to each one of us - to live so as to be missed and to live so that Christ will be magnified. We may be out of step with the world, but we will be in tune and in touch with the Lord. That's exciting!

CHAPTER 15

Dying with Dignity

'Brothers, we do not want you to be ignorant about those who fall asleep, or to grieve like the rest of men, who have no hope. We believe that Jesus died and rose again and so we believe that God will bring with Jesus those who have fallen asleep in him. According to the Lord's own word, we tell you that we who are still alive, who are left till the coming of the Lord, will certainly not precede those who have fallen asleep' (4:13-15)

Two main ideas have been floated in this particular chapter - Paul has been talking about the practical results of Christianity (verses 1-12) and the personal return of Christ (verses 13 -18). It's a chapter of truly remarkable contrasts. For example:

· part one talks about life - part two speaks about death,
· part one is all about the here and now - part two is all about the there and then,
· part one is thinking about time - part two is exploring eternity,
· in part one the challenge is to those who are wide awake - in part two the comfort is for those who have fallen asleep.

He's talking about living well and dying well!

To live well means we will be walking in holiness, harmony and honesty. To die well means we will be embracing a hope, a hope that one day we will see the King in all His beauty.

On the one hand, we have a church energised in the Spirit, the people of God radiating holiness; on the other hand, we have a church expectant in the world, the people of God reflecting hope and living in anticipation of the advent of Jesus.

Hope! That's what modern man is searching for. Do you remember the words of Job when he asked the question: *'Where then is my hope? Who can see any hope for me?'* Isn't it wonderful to realise, there is hope!

When we see what is happening all around us as we rapidly draw near to the end of the second millennium we can be driven to the point of despair. Man's dreams have not been fulfilled. His ideals have not been realised. His best laid plans have been shattered. There are times when our back is to the wall, when we have that awful sinking feeling, when we feel like giving up and giving in - that's when we need hope.

The penman of Hebrews talks about *'a better hope'*. It is an anchor for the soul. When the sands of time are sinking and shifting we have a hope that is sure and steadfast. It's sure for it cannot break, it's steadfast for it cannot slip. That's hope with a capital *'H'*. It gives us the encouragement we need to go on with the Lord. It enables us to fire on every cylinder for Jesus. It keeps us going when the burdens are heavy and the battles are hard.

Hope is not a sedative. It's a shot of adrenaline in the veins of the Christian. You see, where there's Christ there's hope. Hope springs eternal in the human breast only when it is focused on Jesus. It is

Christ in me which is my hope of glory. Time destroys many of our hopes as they fade and die. But, the passing of time only makes the hope of the Christian much more glorious. Solomon said: *'The path of the righteous is like the first gleams of dawn, shining ever brighter till the full light of day'* (Proverbs 4:18).

A similar chord is struck in God's encouragement to Jeremiah for whom hope appeared to have all but evaporated. He said: *'For I know the plans I have for you, plans to give you hope and a future'* (29:11). That brand of hope will put a twinkle in your eye and put the sparkle back into your life. It will add a metre to your every footstep. For, we have something to live for today, and so much to look forward to tomorrow. The world hopes for the best, but the Christian has the best hope.

> *There is coming a day when no heartaches shall come,*
> *No more clouds in the sky, no more tears to dim the eye -*
> *All is peace for evermore on that happy golden shore;*
> *What a day, glorious day, that will be.*

Yes, it's all about dying well! Dying with dignity!

He talks about their fear!

The folks in the church were worried, puzzled and perplexed. They were going through agony of mind and deep anguish of heart. They were really anxious and up-tight. Some of their close friends and loved ones had died and they were concerned lest those who had died would miss out at the second advent of Jesus. That's why they were so upset and I think you'll agree it is perfectly understandable. 'The fear of death,' says Charles Swindoll, 'troubles our lives like a hurricane sweeping over a serene harbour. And, anchored in the shallows, our little boats of faith are easily dashed against the rocks by fear's fury.'

The problem was that their fear was based on ignorance. That explains why Paul says what he does in the opening phrase. Actually this is one of four key areas about which Paul indicates ignorance is not bliss. The others are in 1 Corinthians 10:1 with regard to events in the Old Testament, Romans 11:25 in relation to the ultimate restoration of Israel, and 1 Corinthians 12:1 where he is talking about the manifestation of spiritual gifts.

Here he's talking about death. It's usually the last thing we want to talk about. It makes us feel uncomfortable and awkward. We naturally recoil when someone brings the subject up. And yet, life being what it is, we can't walk away from it. It's an unwelcome intruder into our lives, an uninvited visitor into our homes. It's the king of terrors and the terror of kings. It is man's last great enemy.

The Bible uses many metaphors for death and each one demonstrates the true character of death. For example:

·   death is a snare - *'The fear of the Lord is a fountain of life turning a man from the snares of death'* (Proverbs 14:27)
·   death is a sorrow - David admitted, *'The sorrows of death entangled me'* (Psalm 18:4)
·   death is a shadow - Isaiah reminds us of those *'living in the land of the shadow of death'* (9:2)
·   death is a sting - Paul challenged death when he asked, *'Where, O death, is your sting?'* (1 Corinthians 15:55)
·   death is sleep - that's the reference here in verse 13.

Sleep is something temporary and transient. It is fleeting and passing. When a Christian dies they have fallen asleep in Jesus. They are waiting for the dawning of a new day and longing for the resurrection morning. The body is laid to rest and after the evening of rest there will come the morning of rejoicing. When they pass away and are taken from us, we say *Good Night.* But, when we meet again, we will greet each other with the immortal words, *Good Morning.*

He gave them an illustration in using the metaphor of sleep. He follows up with a word of instruction. Paul knows when we lose a loved one that we will sorrow, we will miss them, we will feel it keenly. There's a vacant chair in the corner, an empty feeling in the life and the heart throbs. Memories linger. But it's only for a wee while, a short time.

When you look at the unsaved, the person who doesn't know the Lord as Saviour, they live and die, without God and without hope. How sad! It's both tragic and devastating! When a Christian dies they go to be with Christ which is immeasurably better. What a marked contrast.

The high priestly prayer of Jesus in John 17:24 is answered at the homecall of every believer. There, in the upper room, he interceded to his Father and said: *'Father, I want those you have given me to be with me where I am, and to see my glory'.*

He talks about a foundation!

Paul declares quite emphatically in verse 14: *'we believe'.* Believe in what? Jesus has died and he has risen again! Here are facts that can't be altered or amended. Here is something which is sure, stable and solid. It is a glorious certainty. It cannot be moved or shaken as these are cardinal truths. They are the central points of our faith. Yes, we say 'Amen' to it. He died and he rose again!

So what? Says Paul, *'because of this, we believe'* - that's what happened to Christ and the same will happen to those of us who know him and love him. Down here we are meant to walk in his footsteps. He died on the cross but that was not the end of the story as on the third day he rose again! For you and for me, we will die, but thank God, we shall rise also.

Christ is the firstfruits (cf. 1 Corinthians 15) - this is the token that one day the harvest will be gathered home. What a memorable day that will be. Bodies will rise from the earth to be reunited with the soul and we shall meet the Lord! According to 1 Peter 1:3 and Romans 8:23 we are waiting for the redemption of the body. Herein lies our assurance, our confidence. That's our hope!

He talks about a fact!

In verse 15 he is at pains to remind them again that this is not a figment of his fertile imagination. Neither is he leading them up the proverbial garden path. This is *'the word of the Lord'*. That suggests:

·   it carries authority,
·   it is authentic,
·   it is totally reliable,
·   it is utterly credible.

He then goes on to draw attention to the two types of people who will be affected with the return of Jesus Christ. There are, those who are alive and those who are asleep!

Christ is coming soon and suddenly. It may be today. His advent is imminent and impending. The Lord is at hand as he could come back at any moment. Our redemption is nearer today than it was when we first placed our trust in him. He is standing at the threshold waiting for the final signal from the Father. It's as close as that!

We could be the generation alive when he breaks through the clouds. If we are, we will not experience death! It's happened before, you know! Remember Enoch - when his walk with the Lord had ended, he left this world not by the dark tunnel of death but by the golden bridge of translation. Remember Elijah - when his work was done, it was instant glory.

When you put them both together you can say with the hymn:

> *When labour's ended and the journey's done*
> *Then He will lead me safely to my home.*

Or,   *Oh joy, oh delight, should we go without dying.*

The facts have got to be faced. There are millions and millions of God's dear people, choice saints, who have gone on before us. They have died. Will they miss out at the second coming of Jesus? That was the question they were grappling with in the early church!

See the privilege that is theirs! And deservedly so. Yes, they will rise. And, they will rise first! They don't miss out as God never short changes his people. They will have the place of honour when the roll is called up yonder. They have caught an earlier train to the final destination of glory. Today we're standing on the station platform. Who knows, but we may be next!

This is what dying with dignity is all about. It's being ready to go when the special moment arrives. We go through the valley of the shadow with our hand in his. He takes us through into the full light of his presence into a land of fadeless day. He leads us into a place where there is fullness of joy and eternal pleasures to be enjoyed. That's exciting, isn't it! Yes, whether we live or whether we die, we are the Lord's.

CHAPTER 16

Advent Adventure

'For the Lord himself will come down from heaven, with a loud command, with the voice of the archangel and with the trumpet call of God, and the dead in Christ will rise first. After that, we who are still alive and are left will be caught up with them in the clouds to meet the Lord in the air. And so we will be with the Lord for ever. Therefore encourage each other with these words' (4:16-18)

Maranatha' was the customary greeting in the early church. Down the street, in the market, across the fence, when God's people met one another this was what they invariably said! It means: *the Lord is coming.*

Two thousand years have come and gone since he made the promise to his disciples in the upper room. So much has happened across the world. Today we are at the eleventh hour and time is fast running out. The signs of the times tell us it can't be long. The countdown is getting lower every day. We need to always remember that the prophetic clock is synchronised with God's time. It ticks steadily forward at its own pace, with its own schedules to keep. This is the next great event on God's prophetic calendar. Lift off for glory is number one on God's agenda for the church. This is the moment when millions will be missing. It is the believer's ultimate trip.

This is something to really look forward to with heightened expectancy in our hearts. Is it any wonder Paul finishes the chapter by saying in verse 18 that this should be a means of mutual encouragement within the family of God.

It means:

· when the going is tough, we can say, hang in there for Christ is coming
· when we feel beaten in the fight, we can say, one day we shall overcome for Christ is coming
· when we feel rejected and of no use to the Lord, we can say, don't lose heart for Christ is coming
· when we say farewell to a loved one and life doesn't seem worth living, we can say, look it won't be long now, for Christ is coming!

Ah, this is not a cop-out experience. It's not an opt out clause either. It's not adopting the ostrich mentality of burying our head in the sand. It's not saying, 'stop the world I want to get off'. What is it then? It's looking forward with hope, excitement, fervour, and bated breath. Christ is coming and that means there is better on before. The best is yet to be. The grave is not our goal for we're born and bound for glory.

When we examine the teaching of the apostle in verses 16 and 17 it is important to note that he is drafting out a programme, drawing up a schedule. There are no fewer than six characteristics surrounding this wonderfully exciting event.

It is personal!

The one returning is the Lord himself. An angel will not be sent in his place as a last minute substitute. There will be no other representative from the Godhead despatched - it will be a personal visit by Jesus. The message he shared with his disciples in the upper room underlines this fact. There he told them: *'I will come again'* (John 14:3). A similar message was echoed by the angels on Ascension Day when they said: *'This same Jesus, who has been taken from you into heaven, will come back in the same way you have seen him go into heaven'* (Acts 1:11).

It is powerful!

There are three welcome sounds associated with the advent of Jesus.

· The sound of the shout - this is a military expression and indicates a command or an order that is given. He will speak with the voice that awakes the dead. In fact, three times in the New Testament do we read of him raising his voice to the level of a shout and each time it is followed by a resurrection. The first is at the grave of Lazarus in John 11 when after he spoke Lazarus emerged as large as life. It's probably fair comment to say that if he hadn't singled Lazarus out for special attention he would have emptied the cemetery! The second was on the cross at Calvary when in triumph he shouted, *'it is finished'* - Matthew's account indicates that graves were opened and many of the saints arose (cf. 27:50). And, the final occasion is right here - again, he will shout and an innumerable company will rise and enter into his immediate presence.

· The activity of the archangel - Michael can be described as the chief prince of the hosts of heaven. He is number one in the angelic pecking order and has a varying range of responsibilities. In Jude 9 he is involved in the realm of controversy in relation to the whereabouts of the body of Moses; in Daniel 12 and Revelation 12 he is hailed as the defender of the nation of Israel in a role of conquest; in Daniel 10 he is to the fore in the realm of conflict especially as it is linked to the problem of unanswered prayer. His participation here is a signal to a watching world that the hordes of hell will have been defeated, death will have lost her sting, and the grave will not have gained the victory. This is the moment when Heaven breaks off diplomatic relations with planet earth as the nationals of Heaven are summoned home.

· The triumph of the trump - this is the last trump as mentioned in 1 Corinthians 15:52. When the silver trumpets were sounded in the Old Testament it was a call to worship, to walk or to war. When the trumpet sounds in that great day *'unto him will the gathering of the people be'*. Then will be held the assembly of the firstborn in the air as many sons will have been brought home to glory. He is the gatherer historically (Mark 4:1) and congregationally (Matthew 18:20). He will be the gatherer universally (Ephesians 1:10) and adventually (as in our present study).

It is purposeful!

Sometimes we ask ourselves the question: why is he coming? Well, here's the answer. For you and me! First of all, the dead; then, the living. He's coming to snatch the saints away - the one who in a moment of time plucked us as brands from the burning will in that final day pluck us out of this world. He will claim us for himself and move us into a new place for eternal habitation. This is all entailed in the phrase employed by John in Revelation 20:5 when he speaks of the first resurrection. It is interesting to note that there are three phases to this particular activity which correspond to the Jewish harvest. They spoke of the time when the firstfruits were reaped and presented to the Lord, then the harvest was gathered home, followed by the picking up of the gleanings. In relation to our Lord's programme this would remind us of the firstfruits being gathered in at his resurrection, the harvest will take place at the moment outlined above and the gleanings will be collected at various times during the period of the tribulation.

It is practical!

What a wonderful day it will be for the people of God for it is then
that *'we shall be changed'*. It will happen in a moment, in the
twinkling of an eye - as fast as that, we will be given a brand new
body. We will be fitted out for glory in clothing which will have
God's designer label attached to it. This body of humiliation will
become a body of glorification, this mortal frame will put on
immortality, and this which is presently corruptible will put on
incorruption - in other words, we will be like Jesus. The work of
sanctification which commenced at the moment of conversion will
then be complete. The good work he begun within our hearts when
we handed our lives over to him will then be finished.

It is precious!

We won't only be like him, we will be with him! The meeting in the
air! It will be a day of glad reunion as we will link up with those
who have gone before us. I'm sure we will know our loved ones in
heaven and together we shall worship the King in all his beauty.
There are many things down here we don't fully understand but then
we will know and it will all make sense. Many questions today are
unanswered but over there all will be made plain. Our dilemma is
that so long as we are down here we see through tinted glass but then
it will be face to face.

It is permanent!

How long will it last? Is it for a day, a week, a month or maybe even
a year? No! It is forever with the Lord. It is eternal. It is bliss
unending. Pleasures for evermore. That's the icing on the cake for
we will be with the one we love. What a consummation! What

communion! What a Christ!

Each day is one day nearer. Each step is one step closer. Perhaps today!

CHAPTER 17

When the Darkness Deepens

'Now, brothers, about times and dates we do not need to write to you, for you know very well that the day of the Lord will come like a thief in the night. While people are saying, "Peace and safety", destruction will come on them suddenly, as labour pains on a pregnant woman, and they will not escape. But you, brothers, are not in darkness so that this day should surprise you like a thief. You are all sons of the light and sons of the day. We do not belong to the night or to the darkness. So then, let us not be like others, who are asleep, but let us be alert and self-controlled. For those who sleep, sleep at night, and those who get drunk, get drunk at night. But since we belong to the day, let us be self-controlled, putting on faith and love as a breastplate, and the hope of salvation as a helmet. For God did not appoint us to suffer wrath but to receive salvation through our Lord Jesus Christ. He died for us so that, whether we are awake or asleep, we may live together with him. Therefore encourage one another and build each other up, just as in fact you are doing' (5:1-11)

We are moving now into the final chapter in Paul's letter to the thriving young church in Thessalonica. Like them, we can be excited and enthusiastic about our Lord Jesus. When we are, it is infectious and contagious. Our zeal and zest for God will rub off on those around us. People will sit up and take notice. They know when we are on the boil for Jesus. That's what this letter is all about. One of the big influences will be our fervent belief in the soon return of Jesus Christ. It's something Paul talks about in every chapter as he says: 'I want you to live your life in the future tense'. Prophecy is never meant to be an end in itself. The purpose of prophetic truth is not speculation, it's motivation - the end times should cause us to shuffle our priorities in the present times. His coming should compel us to share the gospel more urgently, to serve him more faithfully, and to give ourselves to others more freely. It is designed to light a fire under our lives and fan the flame of godly living.

Yes, the message of the second coming of Christ should affect us. But, when you look at the opening verses in this chapter it is fairly obvious that it will have a profound effect upon those who are left behind when Jesus comes. For the Christian a new day is dawning. For the sinner the night is falling and the darkness is deepening.

Phase One of the advent programme of Jesus is when he comes to the air for his people. Phase Two is when he comes to the earth with his people. Stage One is the parousia of Christ. Stage Two is the revelation of Christ. Paul shows us here what happens between the two phases of his return.

A crisis facing the sinner!

Paul begins verse one by saying, *'now, brothers'* which is an indication that he is about to introduce a brand new subject. He is turning a corner as he wants to look at coming events from a fresh perspective and different direction.

He then mentions *'times and dates'* which is an interesting little phrase. It only appears three times in the word of God e.g. Daniel 2:21, Acts 1:7 and here in 1 Thessalonians 5. When our Lord used the term in Acts 1 it was in reference to Israel not to the church of Jesus Christ. It speaks about the coming kingdom. That's why Paul says: *'concerning times and dates we do not need to write to you'.*

He goes on to talk about *'the day of the Lord'* and its significance. This is a most intriguing phrase as it pops up all over the place especially in the prophetic section of the Old Testament. You read about it in Isaiah, Jeremiah, Joel, Amos, Zephaniah and Zechariah. It is also mentioned in the gospels of Matthew and Luke and again by John in the Revelation. So, it's a biblical term, a scriptural expression.

There are many *days* mentioned on the pages of scripture. For example:

- *'days of Jesus life on earth'* (Hebrews 5:7) - from Bethlehem to Calvary
- *'day of salvation'* (2 Corinthians 6:2) - that's now, the age of the grace of God
- *'day of Christ'* (Philippians 1:6) - is a reference to the millennium which is one thousand years of Jesus ruling and reigning on earth
- *'day of God'* (2 Peter 3:12) - speaks of eternity.

The *'day of the Lord'* is the period of Tribulation on earth between the two stages of the coming of Christ. It is designed to last about seven years. Jeremiah describes it as the time of Jacob's trouble. The evangelical prophet Isaiah sees it as the day of vengeance of our God. John later refers to it as the day of wrath of the Lamb. It is the prophet Joel who portrays it as a great and terrible day. It seems that this will be a time slot of frightening and spine chilling events. It is a day of unprecedented happenings which you can read all about in Matthew 24 and in Revelation chapters 6 to 19. It's scary, to say the least! Here is the fate of planet earth in the day when he rises to shake the nations.

The suddenness of such a moment is presented to us with vivid clarity as Paul says it will come *'like a thief in the night'*. We don't know when a thief is coming. We don't really expect a thief to come. We don't sit up and wait for a thief to come. He just comes! It happens, and that's that! The thought here is of a people who are unprepared and who never really expect it to take place in the first instance.

Christ comes when the trumpet sounds and the Christians are immediately translated to glory. The Holy Spirit is removed and the Man of Sin is revealed. And, the world is taken by surprise as man is caught napping. They failed to hear the word of God and they failed to heed the warnings from God.

The seriousness of the day is intimated when the apostle describes it as a time of delusion for they will be saying *'peace and safety'* when in reality there is none. It will be conspicuous by its absence. Anything there is will be transitory in nature and will not last for long. It is also hailed as a time of darkness in every sense of the word. Morally and spiritually it will be an era when the heart of man will be as black as coal. In the natural world there will be certain phenomena as hinted in Joel 2 which will cause a measure of darkness - the sun, moon and stars will withdraw their shining. It is unquestionably a time of destruction. This will be a repeat of the holocaust, only worse! All will reach a climax at Armageddon - World War 3. The conflict of the ages will focus attention on the devastating consequence of man's decision to ignore the pleadings of God's Spirit to trust his Son.

There is a suggestiveness about the day as Paul elaborates further by likening it to *'labour pains on a pregnant woman'*. Jesus himself likened the early days of this period to the beginning of sorrows. Times will be bad but they will escalate out of hand so rapidly. The world and global affairs will appear to be out of control. It is a time of judgment from God on the nations of the world. However, after this and after the purging of the nation of Israel, there will be born the age of the kingdom. There will be weeping and pain for a handful of years. Then Christ will come in phase two of his advent programme and after a night of seven years joy will come in the morning. Oh yes, there are dark days ahead for planet earth and, for the sinner, the worst is yet to come!

A contrast from the scriptures!

The difference between the groups of people Paul is talking about is crystal clear from the terms that he employs. It is true in every case to say that there are only two kinds of people in the world - there are those who know the Lord and there are those who don't. There are saints and sinners and no-one else! It's a 'them and us' situation.

· He speaks of them as *'you'* - he refers to the others as *'those'*
· we are *'sons of the light'* - they *'belong to the darkness'*
· we are *'sons of the day'* - they *'belong to the night'*.

There is a difference in the here and now but there is an incredible difference in the there and then (see verse 9). The Christian will never experience wrath as we have been chosen by grace to receive salvation. The Christian will never know wrath as we have been appointed to know him. That takes you right back to chapter one of the epistle and the doctrine of election. That's the only way to escape the coming judgment.

A challenge for the saints!

Paul pulls no punches as he tells it like it is. He's straight to the point - he goes for the jugular every time. He says, *'We're ready to go to heaven, but are we ready to meet the Lord?'* How can we reach such a state of preparedness?

· Be awake - we are not meant to be sleeping saints! There is no room for apathy. We need to snap out of our lethargy and be delivered from becoming lazy or complacent. This is not the time to be resting on our laurels. Our purpose for living is not to accumulate wealth or make a name for ourselves but to use our abilities to the full in the will of the Lord. We need to get serious.

· Be alert - we should be living on a constant state of red alert. Vigilance is the operative word in this context. Our eyes should be wide open so that we may be able to lead lives that are balanced. The thought here is of someone who has a calm outlook on life. That kind of person hears tragic news but he doesn't lose heart, he experiences difficulties but he doesn't give up, he knows his future is secure in God's hands. You've probably heard it said that the world can be divided into three categories: the few who make things happen, the many who watch things happen, and the vast majority who have no idea what in the world is happening. Paul warns us not to be categorised by the ignorance of the masses, but to always be alert!

The contrast is patently obvious when you look at the unconverted person. They are said to be like drunken men who are living in a stupor. They are enmeshed in a fools false paradise oblivious to the realities of what lies before them. They enjoy a temporary sense of security.

· Be armoured - they are to wake up, get up, clean up and dress up! The armour that has been provided is designed to protect us. Faith and love are like a breastplate which will cover the heart. It is faith toward God and a love for the people of God. Hope is a helmet that protects the mind. In Ephesians 6 it was the *helmet of salvation.* Here in verse 9 it is the *hope of salvation as a helmet.* What is our hope? It is the inescapable fact that one day he is returning.

· Be alive - because he died for us. Whether we live or die we can enjoy the presence of the Lord. That's life with a capital 'L'. Paul is encouraging us to live with eternity in view. This is what living expectantly is all about - it is living in the future tense!

To the Christian there is a distinct message - don't be indifferent today because tomorrow is secure. To the non-Christian there is an equally forthright message - don't be fooled because today seems calm as there is a gathering storm on the horizon.

CHAPTER 18

Looking to the Leadership

'Now we ask you, brothers, to respect those who work hard among you, who are over you in the Lord and who admonish you. Hold them in the highest regard in love because of their work. Live in peace with each other. And we urge you, brothers, warn those who are idle, encourage the timid, help the weak, be patient with everyone. Make sure that nobody pays back wrong for wrong, but always try to be kind to each other and to everyone else' (5:12-15)

The theme that Paul is developing in this short section is of immense importance to the church at Thessalonica - and to the rest of us two thousand years down the road. It is so practical and down to earth that it takes the wind out of our sails. He gives us guidelines to follow that will enable us to maintain a purity in our fellowship.

It's not just a matter of believing sound doctrine, of crossing our theological *Ts,* and of preaching the whole counsel of God. It's more! Our lives should be a reflection of the beauty and loveliness of Jesus. God could have used mirrors to reflect his person, but he didn't. He could have sent angels to reveal his character, but he didn't. He gave that privilege to his children, to you and to me. Therefore, we should be examples of godliness to those around us. So Paul here indicates to us how fellowship can be deepened and damaged. He shows us that we have a responsibility to each other in the Lord because we are members of the same family.

So, says Paul, when we opt out of our responsibilities to each other, when we neglect to care for each other with a heartfelt compassion, when we ignore the principles God has set down, how sad it all is! Each of us is like a wheelbarrow full of loose bricks - dependent on the skilful hands of others to build us up, to help us see the clear-cut truth of God's love. We're meant to be brothers and sisters, bonded in Christ. We are family!

Let's face it, no family is perfect. And, dare I say it, no church is perfect either!

There are problems in every company of the Lord's people. Some are more serious than others. Some appear to be trivial and insignificant. Others look as though they are insurmountable. But, whatever the problem, we are still part of a family.

A happy family is a priceless blessing. What are the essentials for a happy church family? What are the ingredients for an exciting church? Where there is love, care and understanding, mutual help, respect and discipline - all of these and more combine to bring joy in the family of God.

How will this be seen? It will be evident in our attitudes to one another, in the various activities we are involved in, and in our affinity with the Lord Jesus. That is why Paul moves slowly into verses 12 to 15. He deals tactfully and tenderly with two main areas of truth which are both sensitive issues. He handles the obvious difficulties with a delicate touch. He's talking about our conduct and composure in the local church.

·   In verses 12,13 he addresses the matter of our regard for rulers.

· In verses 14,15 he explores the question of our behaviour among the brethren.

God has ordained leadership for every assembly of his people. That's why we have elders and deacons - men who can lead the flock of God. Those involved in leadership roles should be men of vision who are adaptable to the changing needs in a given situation. They should have spiritual discernment and be those who can make and take decisions. We're talking here about men who will act and not always react. Men who will lead from the front and still retain the servant spirit. They should be men of prayer whose lives are in touch and in tune with the Lord. Men who have a heart for God and for his people. We're looking for men of the word!

When we have good, godly and gifted men in such positions of leadership we should respond to them in a three fold manner:

We should respect them!

There are two important phrases in verse 12 which provide the basis for such a healthy respect. It speaks of them being *'among you'* and *'over you'* - the underlying concept is this: as a leader they are over us, but as a brother they are among us! Our respect for them should be based on the fact that even though they are leaders they are still our brothers.

· We should respect them because of their activity - those in leadership are meant to be workers, not passengers. They are supposed to be on the field of play not on the terraces as a cheering or complaining supporter. The implication is that they should be those who *'work hard'* - this is a service that at times can be so wearisome as we seek to care for the souls of men and women. There are tears as well as joys. There are many ups and downs. There is that which is conducted up front but often there is so much more carried out behind the scenes.

- We should respect them because of their authority - this is the argument of the writer in Hebrews 13:7,17 - those who exercise leadership of a pastoral nature have a solemn responsibility. Among other duties they are to feed the flock with the word of God, they are to lead the flock by example and testimony, they are to plead for the flock before the throne of grace. They have the role of an overseer in that they watch over people. Here is one who is in touch with God, with reality and with the people to whom he is called to minister. He will be looking to see how they are getting along. That means going after the sheep that have strayed, picking up the sheep that have been wounded. It means a life invested in others. Why should we do it? One day leaders will give an account and they want to do it with joy rather than it be a burden.

- We should respect them because of their admonition - compare Hebrews 13:7 - an elder or a leader will always be able and willing to sit down with the people of God and open up the word to them. The picture here is of a ministry where people are reminded personally and corporately of the truth of the word of the Lord.

We should esteem them!

Verse 13 indicates that we should appreciate them for what they do for us and we should show our affection for them in the Lord. Why should there be such a total response from the hearts of God's people? Firstly, their gift is from the Lord; and, secondly, a pastor is God's gift to his church (cf. Ephesians 4:11-13). Those in leadership should not be taken for granted. We should endeavour to see the goodness and grace of God in their lives and do all in our power to encourage them.

We should thank God for them!

This is the thought behind Paul's comment at the end of verse 13 where he says: *'live in peace with each other'.* We won't always agree with those in leadership, we won't always see eye to eye with them. There may be things they do or don't do that we don't like. That doesn't matter! We still owe it to them and to the family and to the Lord to thank God for them. We do so because of what they are and who they are!

You get all sorts of sheep in a flock! And, you certainly get all kinds of people in the fellowship. There is the famous trio of yelpers, helpers and skelpers! They have been described as the wise, the unwise and the otherwise. In verses 12 and 13 the focus has been on the leaders; now, he's talking about the rest of us and them as well as he reminds us that we all have a ministry to one another. This is how the body of Christ is meant to function. We're a family and we're all in it together. There are four commands given in verse 14 which we would do well to follow:

· *'warn those who are idle'* - he's talking here about those who are careless, who are out of step, out of line. These are the individuals who are breaking rank. They are to be reprimanded in love. There's a place to do it, there's a time to do it, and there's a way to do it. (Compare what he says in his second letter in 3:6,11). If there is no change of heart then we have no alternative but to withdraw from them. These are the hard hearted people in the fellowship - the won't do's!

· *'encourage the timid'* - this means we are to come alongside and near to those saints who get down in the dumps rather easily. We are to encourage those who are prone to give up and give in - we are to try to lift them up. There are always quitters in every family but it's always too soon to quit! There are those who perpetually look on the dark side and Paul encourages us to show them the light. These are the faint hearted folks in the church - the want to's!

· *'help the weak'* - ours is a support ministry as the reference here is to those who are weak in the faith. They have not grown up in their relationship with the Lord. They are still on the milk when they should be eating the meat. To all such, we should hold on to them, bear them up, care for them, stand by them and with them. These are the dear friends who are broken hearted - the can't do's!

· *'be patient with everyone'* - Paul's a realist. He knows this will not be easy. It's tough. There will be times when you're at your limit, when you've had enough. We are to be patient and give them time and show them Jesus. We are to be long tempered rather than being like a short fuse. It's all about self-control.

We are to watch our motives! Yes, this is what happens in a family and in a church. It's human nature. By the same token, it's sinful. We should never retaliate and try to get even with a brother or sister. We should be ultra careful what we return to them. The temptation is for us to get our own back, to stand up for our rights and to settle old scores. Well, that's not the way of Christ! We should endeavour to be kind and only do what is good as this is the only way to overcome evil. Two wrongs never make one right! We should show something to them of the love of Jesus and remember that God always has the last word. He alone writes the last chapter. Therefore, we should be content to leave it all with him.

CHAPTER 19

Glorying in God

'Be joyful always; pray continually; give thanks in all circumstances, for this is God's will for you in Christ Jesus. Do not put out the Spirit's fire; do not treat prophecies with contempt. Test everything. Hold on to the good. Avoid every kind of evil' (5:16-22)

We are meant to enjoy life not endure it! Here are seven sayings that can give you a life that is permeated with joy and zest. The most magnetic people on earth should be those in the family of God - for their experience of the grace of God should be both exciting and contagious. We have something to sing and shout about. We have every reason to be infectious in our enthusiasm for the Lord.

Sadly, for so many of God's people, life appears to be one big long bore. Their most exciting encounter is found on the soap opera beamed into their home from some television company. It's the highlight of their week! Well, if that's the case, they're the ones who are really missing out. This section reminds us that we can experience life to the full if we embrace these seven pertinent and pithy sayings.

A life in tune with God!

'Be joyful always' is the shortest verse in the Greek New Testament.

It means we have something the world hasn't got. We have a joy deep down in our hearts. Some Christians have a joy that is so deep it never rises to the surface. Happiness depends on what happens to us and what is taking place around us - but this joy is centred in Jesus. Our circumstances change, the tide ebbs and flows, our fortunes fluctuate, life can be like the proverbial yo-yo, yet we can still have joy all of the time.

We read of Christ giving to us his grace, his peace, and here it is his joy. This blessing is ours when we abide in him (cf. John 15). When our lives are lived in the fulness of the Holy Spirit then joy is the fruit that is manifest. We can cheer up for there's joy in Jesus.

A life in touch with God!

When we talk about praying continually it underlines the necessity of keeping short accounts with the Lord. The idea here is not of round the clock praying but of keeping in touch with God. It is keeping the lines of communication open. It is keeping the channels clear. It is living in the atmosphere of Christ and breathing the air of heaven. It is being able to converse and chat with him at any time of the day or night. It's a hotline to heaven!

It is living in the reality of Psalm 91:1 when we abide under the shadow of the Almighty. Such moments are times when we sense his nearness, when we live in the place where God answers prayer. It is when there is nothing between our hearts and heaven.

He's only a prayer away, he sees your every sigh, he hears every sob, he is familiar with every sentence you utter - that's what fellowship is all about.

It's when we get rid of the burdens as we give them over to him. Then we find release in our hearts and joy abounds. Prayer can free us from the anchors of life that drag us down and drain our joy. He is El Shaddai, the God who is enough! That's exciting!

A life of trust in God!

When we give thanks in all circumstances we are using the gift and grace of contentment. We are happy with our lot. It is thanks not *for* everything but *in* everything. For example, remember Paul and Silas in prison in Philippi. Whether we find ourselves in the storm or in the calm, in deep waters or on dry land, it matters not for his plan is designed for our good. This is living in the reality of Romans 8:28 and it enables us to say 'thankyou' for every experience he brings into our lives. The bottom line is that we submit willingly to his sovereignty with an overwhelming sense of gratitude.

A life on top for God!

The Holy Spirit is a friend so we may grieve him when we hurt him. Here in verse 19 he is likened to a fire which means that we may quench him when we suppress and stifle his influence in our lives. The danger is that we may try to extinguish him in our lives and in the lives of others. It is foolish to pour cold water on his plan for our lives or even to dampen the effect of his word upon our hearts.

The fire burns up the dross in that it purifies. It has incredible power so that it brings light and gives warmth. We need to be touched with a live coal from off the altar and be a people ignited for the Lord. We need to burn for the Lord in such a manner that people will be aware that we are ablaze for him. It was Amy Carmichael who prayed: "Make me thy fuel, O flame of God".

A life being taught by God!

When God is speaking to his people we should be extra cautious about our response. We must never downgrade the word from the Lord by displaying a lack of interest in it. When God's word is proclaimed, whatever the channel, we should be treating it as the word of God. It is not the voice of man. It is God who is speaking to us. Let's not get overly familiar with him and his word. When we do we risk bringing contempt to our souls.

A life of testing for God!

There is, especially in these days, a need to examine what is before us by asking the searching question: is it in harmony with the teaching of Scripture? We need spiritual discernment so that we may be able to tell the difference between what is right and what is wrong. The tendency is to write everything that is 'new' off and then throw the baby out with the bath water. We must be prayerful in our approach and balanced in our critique of what is presented to us. Yes, we test it for God, and we hold on to what is good. It's the Berean syndrome as outlined in Acts 17:11.

A life of triumph in God!

Here the apostle is calling God's people to a life of total abstinence. That doesn't just apply to the more obvious 'sins' but to every form of evil. It is not, however, just evil in itself, but the appearance of it! In other words, we should keep ourselves unspotted and untainted from that which is less than desirable around us. Don't get contaminated! Don't allow yourself to become polluted. If there's any doubt, don't dabble in it! We should not give people a chance to talk about us nor should we give them an opportunity to point the finger at us. Many a life has been wasted and many a testimony ruined because of a moment's indiscretion. I suppose we can look at it like this, if you can't take Jesus with you then you shouldn't be there!

CHAPTER 20

Living in the Future Tense

'May God himself, the God of peace, sanctify you through and through. May your whole spirit, soul and body be kept blameless at the coming of our Lord Jesus Christ. The one who calls you is faithful and he will do it. Brothers, pray for us. Greet all the brothers with a holy kiss. I charge you before the Lord to have this letter read to all the brothers. The grace of our Lord Jesus Christ be with you' (5:23-28)

In these final few verses Paul bids them a fond farewell. He just wants to say 'goodbye' to them but that has not been easy for him to do. He found it enormously difficult. Actually, he took six verses to close his letter. Everything he said shows his deep affection for them. He talks about:

· a God who is faithful,
· friends who are loyal,
· grace which is lasting.

The standard that is expected!

Paul turns back in verse 23 to a theme that is near and dear to his heart - holiness of life. He has dealt with it before in the preceding chapter by reminding them that this lifestyle was part and parcel of

God's will for them. These are days when standards are falling, when the enemy has come in like a flood, when the banner of holiness to the Lord is rarely unfurled to the breeze. Yet, God's word has not changed. He expects of each of his children, holiness of life and a godliness in character.

This verse indicates that this deep work in the heart of the Christian is ascribed to God our Father. It's a divine work as he makes us more like Jesus. This is what being conformed to his image is all about.

It is **positional** (cf. Hebrews 10:10) in that we have been once and for all set apart for God. It is **practical** (cf. 2 Corinthians 7:1) in that it is a daily dealing with our sin and a consequent growth in holiness. It is **perfect** (cf. 1 John 3:1-3) for in eternity we will be forever like him.

Paul says here that the expectation in our hearts that one day we will see Jesus should be a spur to holy living. It should be enough to motivate us.

He prays that he might sanctify us *'through and through'* - this is the only time this phrase is used in the New Testament. The underlying thought here is of entire sanctification. According to the apostle it affects *'spirit, soul and body'*. It is when everything is under his influence and control and our lives are yielded to him one hundred percent. It is full surrender and total commitment.

Did you see how he is described in verse 23? We are introduced to him as the *'God of peace'*. When he is not in control of our lives, we are restless, in turmoil, tossed to and fro. But, when he is Lord and is enthroned as King, there is an inner calm, a conscious resting in him, an inner quietness, a real sense of tranquility. There is nothing to disturb or distract. We feel his peace and we know his peace.

The statement that is emphasised!

What a staggering comment we have in verse 24! It is an exceeding great and precious promise. We say, 'We can't live a holy life, we can't keep the standard he has set, it's all too much for us, it's too high for us, we fail miserably so often'.

Paul says, 'Alright, I hear what you're saying, but look to the Lord!'

Why should we turn our eyes toward him?

·   He has called us. The general call in evangelism became personalised when we bowed the knee to Jesus. It became effectual when we said 'yes' to him.

·   He is faithful. His faithfulness is such it reaches even to the mountains. He has remained loyal and true and never once has he let his people down. Never has he gone back on his word. When we needed him most he was always there. He has not, he will not, and he cannot fail us.

·   He is powerful. *'He will do it'* - think of all he has done in the past, think of all that he is doing in the present. If he has done it before and is doing it now then he can do it again.

Why will he do it? He longs that we might be with him in his home for ever. There we shall worship him with clean hands and a pure heart. There we shall see him in the beauty of his holiness. There we shall commune with him in spirit and in truth. A former Archbishop of Canterbury, William Temple, says worship is 'to quicken the conscience by the holiness of God, to feed the mind with the truth of God, to purge the imagination by the beauty of God, to open up the heart to the love of God, and to devote the will to the purpose of God'.

The sharing that is encouraged!

Paul opens his heart here in verses 25,26 with an impassioned plea to the church. He says, *'pray for us'*. How unashamed he is of such a request. How sad he may be at the lack of response. This is what we need today and especially all those involved on the frontline of ministry. Here is the power of effective kneeling.

· Think of his humility - he's a man and he's standing in need of their prayers. He is big enough to know his many shortcomings and he's small enough to beg for their prayerful support.

· Think of his honesty - it's exactly the way he feels. If he didn't he wouldn't have asked. It's genuine, real and sincere.

The customary greeting in the early church was for a man to greet another man with a kiss on the cheek or forehead. It was the same principle for the ladies. Then, it was culturally acceptable as it was the proper thing to do. They were demonstrating their love for each other in the family of God. It was a seal of their affection and a feeling of belonging to one another.

Today, it may be a friendly embrace, a pat on the back, a kiss, a shake of the hand - the method is not important, the motive certainly is! Surely one of the best ways to show others our love is through the acceptance we whisper in a warm touch.

The supply that is experienced!

What a benediction! At the start of the letter, he said, 'Hello, grace to you' - at the end of the letter he says, 'Cheerio, grace be with you!'

The grace of God is something that saves us. It always sustains and strengthens us. It is ever sufficient for us in that it is immeasureable.

It is truly undeserved and unearned. And, the wonderful thing about it is this, it is unrepayable. Why grace?

Chuck Swindoll in his book, *The Grace Awakening,* says: 'What is it that frees us to be all he means us to be? Grace. What is it that permits others to be who they are, even *very* different from us? Grace. What allows us to disagree, yet stimulates us to press on? Grace. What adds oil to the friction points of a marriage, freeing both partners from pettiness and negativism? Grace. And what gives magnetic charm to a ministry, inviting others to become a part? Again ... grace!'

He knew their surroundings, he is familiar with their situation, he is conscious of their problems and difficulties, he is aware of their changing circumstances. And so, he commends them to the grace of God and to the God of all grace.

We have come to the end of the book but the grace of God is lasting and limitless. He says to each of us, 'It's there for you, make the most of it'. When we do, our testimony for the Lord will be contagious and there will be an air of excitement to our relationship with the Saviour. And, it will spill over into our churches as well.

That means: **your church will be exciting too!**